Activity Guide
and Working Papers
BOOK 2 • CHAPTERS 10–20

Financial Management and Recordkeeping

Jeffrey R. Stewart, Ed.D.
Professor of Business Education, Emeritus
Virginia Polytechnic Institute and State University
Blacksburg, Virginia
Currently Educational Consultant

Daisy L. Stewart, Ph.D.
Director, Division of Vocational and Technical Education
Virginia Polytechnic Institute and State University
Blacksburg, Virginia

Harry Huffman, Ed.D.
Late Professor of Business Education
Ohio State University and Colorado State University

GLENCOE
McGraw-Hill

New York, New York   Columbus, Ohio   Woodland Hills, California   Peoria, Illinois

Activity Guide and Working Papers, Book 2
Financial Management and Recordkeeping

Send all inquiries to:
Glencoe/McGraw-Hill
21600 Oxnard St., Suite 500
Woodland Hills, CA 91367-4906

ISBN 0-02-801108-2

Printed in the United States of America

12 13 14 15   066   06 05 04

CHAPTER 10

SALES RECORDS AND REPORTS

TOPIC 1 ● RECORDING RETAIL CHARGE SALES   Textbook pages 278 to 282

Check Your Reading

Use the spaces below to answer the questions on pages 282 to 283 of your textbook.

1. _____

2. _____   **3.** _____

_____   **4.** _____

Exercises for Topic 1

1. Do Exercise 1 on pages 283 to 284 of your textbook. Write your answers below.

a. _____   **c.** _____

b. _____   **d.** _____

_____

2. Do Exercise 2 on page 284 of your textbook. Write your answers on the charge sales slips below and on the next page of your Activity Guide.

a.

	DATE	DEPT.	CLERK NO.	INITIAL	SEND	
					TAKE	
QUAN.	CLASS	ARTICLE		UNIT PRICE	EXTENSION	
				SUB TOTAL		
	AUTHORIZATION CODE			TAX		
				TOTAL		

SALE CONFIRMED AND DRAFT ACCEPTED

b.

	DATE	DEPT.	CLERK NO.	INITIAL	SEND	
					TAKE	
QUAN.	CLASS	ARTICLE		UNIT PRICE	EXTENSION	
				SUB TOTAL		
	AUTHORIZATION CODE			TAX		
				TOTAL		

SALE CONFIRMED AND DRAFT ACCEPTED

c.

		DATE	DEPT.	CLERK NO.	INITIAL	SEND	
						TAKE	
	QUAN.	CLASS	ARTICLE		UNIT PRICE	EXTENSION	
					SUB TOTAL		
					TAX		
		AUTHORIZATION CODE					
					TOTAL		

SALE CONFIRMED AND DRAFT ACCEPTED

d.

		DATE	DEPT.	CLERK NO.	INITIAL	SEND	
						TAKE	
	QUAN.	CLASS	ARTICLE		UNIT PRICE	EXTENSION	
					SUB TOTAL		
					TAX		
		AUTHORIZATION CODE					
					TOTAL		

SALE CONFIRMED AND DRAFT ACCEPTED

3. Do Exercise 3 on page 284 of your textbook. Write your answers below.

a.

		DATE	DEPT.	CLERK NO.	INITIAL	
	QUAN.	CLASS	ARTICLE		UNIT PRICE	EXTENSION
					SUB TOTAL	
		AUTHORIZATION CODE			TAX	
					TOTAL	

SALE CONFIRMED AND DRAFT ACCEPTED

b.

		DATE	DEPT.	CLERK NO.	INITIAL	
	QUAN.	CLASS	ARTICLE		UNIT PRICE	EXTENSION
					SUB TOTAL	
		AUTHORIZATION CODE			TAX	
					TOTAL	

SALE CONFIRMED AND DRAFT ACCEPTED

Name _____

Date _____

TOPIC 2 ● MAINTAINING ACCOUNTS RECEIVABLE Textbook pages 285 to 290

Check Your Reading

Use the spaces below to answer the questions on pages 290 to 291 of your textbook.

1. _____
   _____

2. a. _____
   b. _____
   c. _____

3. _____
   _____

4. _____
   _____

5. _____

6. _____

7. _____
   _____
   _____

Exercises for Topic 2

1. Do Exercise 1 on pages 291 to 292 of your textbook. Use the spaces below to list any errors you find and the corrected amounts. If there are no errors, write "none." Then write the total amount of all six sales slips.

   a. _____
   b. _____
   c. _____
   d. _____
   e. _____
   f. _____

   The total amount of the six sales slips after corrections: _____

2. Do Exercise 2 on page 292 of your textbook. Cross out each incorrect amount on the sales slips below and write the correct amount above it. (Note: The sales tax rate is 4 percent.) Then write the total in the space at the bottom of the page.

Slip 1 — JAMES POST — 7321 766 932

	DATE	DEPT.	CLERK NO.	INITIAL	SEND	
	4/3/—	16	21	L.T.	TAKE	√

QUAN.	CLASS	ARTICLE	UNIT PRICE	EXTENSION	
2	18	Men's shirts	18.99	37	98
			SUB TOTAL	37	98
		AUTHORIZATION CODE	TAX	1	52
			TOTAL	39	50

SALE CONFIRMED AND DRAFT ACCEPTED
✕ James Post

KEENEY'S
CLOTHING STORE
Meadow Walk Mall   Wichita KS
67210

B2463-28

Slip 2 — ELSIE TINWOOD — 2745 838 394

	DATE	DEPT.	CLERK NO.	INITIAL	SEND	
	4/3/—	42	21	L.T.	TAKE	√

QUAN.	CLASS	ARTICLE	UNIT PRICE	EXTENSION	
2	26	Blouses	15.88	31	76
2	34	Skirts	23.44	46	86
			SUB TOTAL	78	62
		AUTHORIZATION CODE	TAX	3	14
			TOTAL	81	75

SALE CONFIRMED AND DRAFT ACCEPTED
✕ Elsie Tinwood

KEENEY'S
CLOTHING STORE
Meadow Walk Mall   Wichita KS
67210

B2464-29

Slip 3 — TOM SEGAL — 6291 493 320

	DATE	DEPT.	CLERK NO.	INITIAL	SEND	
	4/3/—	28	21	L.T.	TAKE	√

QUAN.	CLASS	ARTICLE	UNIT PRICE	EXTENSION	
1	23	Men's suit	159.95	159	95
1	42	Pr. shoes	43.50	43	50
			SUB TOTAL	203	45
		AUTHORIZATION CODE	TAX	10	17
			TOTAL	213	62

SALE CONFIRMED AND DRAFT ACCEPTED
✕ Tom Segal

KEENEY'S
CLOTHING STORE
Meadow Walk Mall   Wichita KS
67210

B2465-30

The total amount of the three sales slips after corrections: _____

Name _____

Date _____

3. Do Exercise 3 on pages 292 to 293 of your textbook. Use the customer account forms below and the forms on pages 6 to 8 of your Activity Guide.

a. and b.

Name _____ Account No._____
Address _____

DATE	EXPLANATION	POST. REF.	DEBIT	CREDIT	BALANCE

Name _____ Account No._____
Address _____

DATE	EXPLANATION	POST. REF.	DEBIT	CREDIT	BALANCE

Name _____ Account No._____
Address _____

DATE	EXPLANATION	POST. REF.	DEBIT	CREDIT	BALANCE

Name _____ Account No._____
Address _____

DATE	EXPLANATION	POST. REF.	DEBIT	CREDIT	BALANCE

c.

Nina's
Fashion Boutique

STATEMENT OF ACCOUNT

CLOSING DATE

DUE DATE

AMOUNT PAID $ [|]

Please detach and return this stub. Your canceled check is your receipt.

Previous Balance	Charges (+)	Credits (−)	Finance Charge (+)	Account Balance	Amount Now Due

Nina's
Fashion Boutique

Payments, returns, and purchases reaching our charge office
after billing date will be shown on your next statement.

Please mail or bring saleschecks and credits when making an inquiry on this statement.

Nina's
Fashion Boutique

STATEMENT OF ACCOUNT

CLOSING DATE

DUE DATE

AMOUNT PAID $ [|]

Please detach and return this stub. Your canceled check is your receipt.

Previous Balance	Charges (+)	Credits (−)	Finance Charge (+)	Account Balance	Amount Now Due

Nina's
Fashion Boutique

Payments, returns, and purchases reaching our charge office
after billing date will be shown on your next statement.

Please mail or bring saleschecks and credits when making an inquiry on this statement.

Name _____

Date _____

Nina's ✿
Fashion Boutique

STATEMENT OF ACCOUNT

CLOSING DATE

DUE DATE

AMOUNT PAID $ [|]

Please detach and return this stub. Your canceled check is your receipt.

Previous Balance	Charges (+)	Credits (−)	Finance Charge (+)	Account Balance	Amount Now Due

Nina's ✿
Fashion Boutique

Payments, returns, and purchases reaching our charge office after billing date will be shown on your next statement.

Please mail or bring saleschecks and credits when making an inquiry on this statement.

Nina's ✿
Fashion Boutique

STATEMENT OF ACCOUNT

CLOSING DATE

DUE DATE

AMOUNT PAID $ [|]

Please detach and return this stub. Your canceled check is your receipt.

Previous Balance	Charges (+)	Credits (−)	Finance Charge (+)	Account Balance	Amount Now Due

Nina's ✿
Fashion Boutique

Payments, returns, and purchases reaching our charge office after billing date will be shown on your next statement.

Please mail or bring saleschecks and credits when making an inquiry on this statement.

d. After each stub has been posted, make a check mark beside the amount paid.

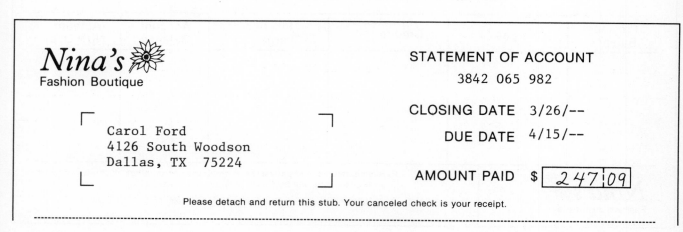

Nina's 🌻
Fashion Boutique

STATEMENT OF ACCOUNT
5036 812 288

CLOSING DATE 3/26/--

DUE DATE 4/15/--

Pauline Bowers
6184 Ninth Avenue
Dallas, TX 75239

AMOUNT PAID $ | 143 | 22 |

Please detach and return this stub. Your canceled check is your receipt.

Nina's 🌻
Fashion Boutique

STATEMENT OF ACCOUNT
3842 065 982

CLOSING DATE 3/26/--

DUE DATE 4/15/--

Carol Ford
4126 South Woodson
Dallas, TX 75224

AMOUNT PAID $ | 247 | 09 |

Please detach and return this stub. Your canceled check is your receipt.

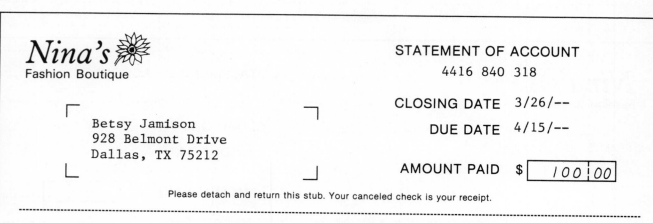

Nina's 🌻
Fashion Boutique

STATEMENT OF ACCOUNT
4416 840 318

CLOSING DATE 3/26/--

DUE DATE 4/15/--

Betsy Jamison
928 Belmont Drive
Dallas, TX 75212

AMOUNT PAID $ | 100 | 00 |

Please detach and return this stub. Your canceled check is your receipt.

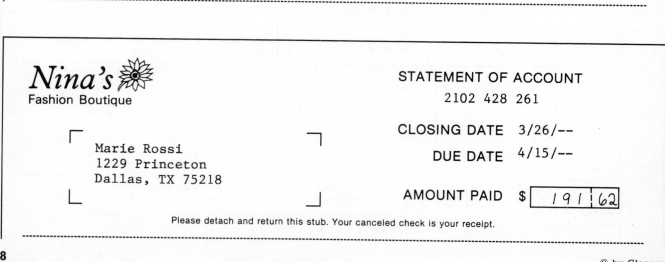

Nina's 🌻
Fashion Boutique

STATEMENT OF ACCOUNT
2102 428 261

CLOSING DATE 3/26/--

DUE DATE 4/15/--

Marie Rossi
1229 Princeton
Dallas, TX 75218

AMOUNT PAID $ | 191 | 62 |

Please detach and return this stub. Your canceled check is your receipt.

8

Name _____

Date _____

TOPIC 3 ● EXAMINING SALES REPORTS   Textbook pages 293 to 296

Check Your Reading

Use the spaces below to answer the questions on page 296 of your textbook.

1. _____

_____

_____

2. _____

3. _____

_____

_____

_____

_____

4. _____

_____

_____

_____

_____

5. _____

_____

_____

Exercises for Topic 3

1. Do Exercise 1 on page 297 of your textbook. Write your answers in the spaces below.

a. _____

_____

_____

b. _____

c. _____

d. _____

e. _____

f. _____

2. Do Exercise 2 on page 297 of your textbook. Write your answers in the spaces below.

a. _____

_____

_____

_____

b. _____

_____

_____

_____

_____

c. _____

_____

_____

3. Do Exercise 3 on page 297 of your textbook. Write your answers in the spaces below.

Department	Percentage Increase	This Year's Sales	Sales Increase	Next Year's Quota
Alloys	4	$174,210	_____	_____
Aluminum	5	214,993	_____	_____
Brass	2	93,208	_____	_____
Chrome plating	1	118,454	_____	_____
Iron casting	4	378,226	_____	_____
Steel milling	5	401,756	_____	_____
Welding	6	124,153	_____	_____
Zinc products	12	63,289	_____	_____

Name _____

Date _____

END OF CHAPTER ACTIVITIES Textbook pages 298 to 302

Math Skillbuilder

Do the Math Skillbuilder on page 298 of your textbook—figuring the extension, subtotal, tax, and total for a sale. Use the spaces below to write your answers.

1. _____

    _____

    _____

  Subtotal _____

  Tax at 4% _____

  Total _____

2. _____

    _____

    _____

  Subtotal _____

  Tax at 4% _____

  Total _____

3. _____

    _____

    _____

    _____

  Subtotal _____

  Tax at 4% _____

  Total _____

4. _____

    _____

    _____

  Subtotal _____

  Tax at 4% _____

  Total _____

5. _____

    _____

    _____

  Subtotal _____

  Tax at 4% _____

  Total _____

6. _____

    _____

    _____

  Subtotal _____

  Tax at 4% _____

  Total _____

7. _____

    _____

    _____

  Subtotal _____

  Tax at 4% _____

  Total _____

8. _____

    _____

  Subtotal _____

  Tax at 4% _____

  Total _____

Do the Math Skillbuilder on page 298 of your textbook—finding the customer's balance, given the beginning balance and a debit or credit amount. Write your answers in the spaces below.

	Debit	Credit	Balance
1.	$100.00	—	_____
2.	—	$ 50.00	_____
3.	55.00	—	_____
4.	—	25.50	_____
5.	—	10.75	_____
6.	75.20	—	_____
7.	17.50	—	_____
8.	—	56.25	_____
9.	48.95	—	_____
10.	—	212.00	_____

Vocabulary Skillbuilder

Do the Vocabulary Skillbuilder on pages 299 to 300 of your textbook. Use the spaces below to write the term that best matches each statement.

1. _____
2. _____
3. _____
4. _____
5. _____
6. _____
7. _____
8. _____
9. _____
10. _____

11. _____
12. _____
13. _____
14. _____
15. _____
16. _____
17. _____
18. _____
19. _____
20. _____

Application Problems

1. Do Problem 1 on page 300 of your textbook. Answer the questions in the spaces below.

   a. _____

   b. _____

   c. _____

   d. _____

2. Do Problem 2 on pages 300 to 301 of your textbook. Use the sales slips and credit memos below and on pages 14 to 16 of your Activity Guide. Write your initials in the "Initial" box at the top of each form.

a.

DATE		DEPT.	CLERK NO.	INITIAL	SEND	
					TAKE	

QUAN.	CLASS	ARTICLE		UNIT PRICE	EXTENSION	
					SUB TOTAL	
					TAX	
	AUTHORIZATION CODE				TOTAL	

36 422 17

TONYA R. WATSON

SALE CONFIRMED AND DRAFT ACCEPTED
✕

Benn's Department Store
Dayton, Ohio 45410

C5634-75

DATE		DEPT.	CLERK NO.	INITIAL	SEND	
					TAKE	

QUAN.	CLASS	ARTICLE		UNIT PRICE	EXTENSION	
					SUB TOTAL	
					TAX	
	AUTHORIZATION CODE				TOTAL	

37 424 71

JILL N. JENSEN

SALE CONFIRMED AND DRAFT ACCEPTED
✕

Benn's Department Store
Dayton, Ohio 45410

C5634-76

	DATE		DEPT.	CLERK NO.	INITIAL	SEND	
						TAKE	
	QUAN.	CLASS		ARTICLE	UNIT PRICE	EXTENSION	
					SUB TOTAL		
			AUTHORIZATION CODE		TAX		
					TOTAL		

37 719 22

FRIEDA G. YOUNOS

SALE CONFIRMED AND DRAFT ACCEPTED

X

Benn's Department Store   **C5634-77**
Dayton, Ohio 45410

	DATE		DEPT.	CLERK NO.	INITIAL	SEND	
						TAKE	
	QUAN.	CLASS		ARTICLE	UNIT PRICE	EXTENSION	
					SUB TOTAL		
			AUTHORIZATION CODE		TAX		
					TOTAL		

40 307 91

WILLETTE D. PRICE

SALE CONFIRMED AND DRAFT ACCEPTED

X

Benn's Department Store   **C5634-78**
Dayton, Ohio 45410

	DATE		DEPT.	CLERK NO.	INITIAL	SEND	
						TAKE	
	QUAN.	CLASS		ARTICLE	UNIT PRICE	EXTENSION	
					SUB TOTAL		
			AUTHORIZATION CODE		TAX		
					TOTAL		

37 424 71

JILL N. JENSEN

SALE CONFIRMED AND DRAFT ACCEPTED

X

Benn's Department Store   **C5634-79**
Dayton, Ohio 45410

14

DATE		DEPT.	CLERK NO.	INITIAL	SEND	
					TAKE	
QUAN.	CLASS	ARTICLE		UNIT PRICE	EXTENSION	
					SUB TOTAL	
					TAX	
	AUTHORIZATION CODE				TOTAL	

36 422 17

TONYA R. WATSON

SALE CONFIRMED AND DRAFT ACCEPTED
X

Benn's Department Store
Dayton, Ohio 45410

C5634-80

DATE		DEPT.	CLERK NO.	INITIAL	SEND	
					TAKE	
QUAN.	CLASS	ARTICLE		UNIT PRICE	EXTENSION	
					SUB TOTAL	
					TAX	
	AUTHORIZATION CODE				TOTAL	

40 307 91

WILLETTE D. PRICE

SALE CONFIRMED AND DRAFT ACCEPTED
X

Benn's Department Store
Dayton, Ohio 45410

C5634-81

DATE		DEPT.	CLERK NO.	INITIAL	SEND	
					TAKE	
QUAN.	CLASS	ARTICLE		UNIT PRICE	EXTENSION	
					SUB TOTAL	
					TAX	
	AUTHORIZATION CODE				TOTAL	

37 719 22

FRIEDA G. YOUNOS

SALE CONFIRMED AND DRAFT ACCEPTED
X

Benn's Department Store
Dayton, Ohio 45410

C5634-82

b.

	DATE	DEPT.	CLERK NO.	INITIAL	
37 719 22					
	QUAN.	CLASS	ARTICLE	UNIT PRICE	EXTENSION
FRIEDA G. YOUNOS				SUB TOTAL	
	AUTHORIZATION CODE			TAX	
				TOTAL	

CUSTOMER'S SIGNATURE
×

Benn's Department Store
Dayton, Ohio 45410

CM 2860
CREDIT MEMORANDUM

	DATE	DEPT.	CLERK NO.	INITIAL	
40 307 91					
	QUAN.	CLASS	ARTICLE	UNIT PRICE	EXTENSION
WILLETTE D. PRICE				SUB TOTAL	
	AUTHORIZATION CODE			TAX	
				TOTAL	

CUSTOMER'S SIGNATURE
×

Benn's Department Store
Dayton, Ohio 45410

CM 2861
CREDIT MEMORANDUM

3. Do Problem 3 on page 301 of your textbook. Use the sales slips and credit memos from Problem 2, the customer account forms on page 17, and the statement of account forms on pages 18 and 19 of your Activity Guide.

a. Review each sales slip and credit memo prepared in Problem 2. See pages 13 to 16 of your Activity Guide. Make any necessary corrections. After you review the slips, initial each in the lower-right corner.

b. Write the amounts figured for the accounting department in the spaces below.

1. _____   4. _____

2. _____   5. _____

3. _____   6. _____

c. Set up the four customer accounts using the forms on page 17 of your Activity Guide.

d. Remember to make a check mark beside the total of each sales slip or credit memo on pages 13 to 16 of your Activity Guide after you have posted the item.

e. The statement of account forms are on pages 18 and 19 of your Activity Guide.

f. Post each cash receipt to the correct account.

c., d., and f.

Name _____ Account No. _____

Address _____

DATE	EXPLANATION	POST. REF.	DEBIT	CREDIT	BALANCE

Name _____ Account No. _____

Address _____

DATE	EXPLANATION	POST. REF.	DEBIT	CREDIT	BALANCE

Name _____ Account No. _____

Address _____

DATE	EXPLANATION	POST. REF.	DEBIT	CREDIT	BALANCE

Name _____ Account No. _____

Address _____

DATE	EXPLANATION	POST. REF.	DEBIT	CREDIT	BALANCE

e.

Benn's Department Store
Dayton, Ohio 45410

STATEMENT OF ACCOUNT

CLOSING DATE

DUE DATE

AMOUNT PAID $

Please detach and return this stub. Your canceled check is your receipt.

Previous Balance	Charges (+)	Credits (−)	Finance Charge (+)	Account Balance	Amount Now Due

Benn's Department Store
Dayton, Ohio 45410

Payments, returns, and purchases reaching our charge office
after billing date will be shown on your next statement.

Please mail or bring saleschecks and credits when making an inquiry on this statement.

Benn's Department Store
Dayton, Ohio 45410

STATEMENT OF ACCOUNT

CLOSING DATE

DUE DATE

AMOUNT PAID $

Please detach and return this stub. Your canceled check is your receipt.

Previous Balance	Charges (+)	Credits (−)	Finance Charge (+)	Account Balance	Amount Now Due

Benn's Department Store
Dayton, Ohio 45410

Payments, returns, and purchases reaching our charge office
after billing date will be shown on your next statement.

Please mail or bring saleschecks and credits when making an inquiry on this statement.

Benn's Department Store
Dayton, Ohio 45410

STATEMENT OF ACCOUNT

CLOSING DATE

DUE DATE

AMOUNT PAID $ [|]

Please detach and return this stub. Your canceled check is your receipt.

Previous Balance	Charges (+)	Credits (−)	Finance Charge (+)	Account Balance	Amount Now Due

Benn's Department Store
Dayton, Ohio 45410

Payments, returns, and purchases reaching our charge office after billing date will be shown on your next statement.

Please mail or bring saleschecks and credits when making an inquiry on this statement.

Benn's Department Store
Dayton, Ohio 45410

STATEMENT OF ACCOUNT

CLOSING DATE

DUE DATE

AMOUNT PAID $ [|]

Please detach and return this stub. Your canceled check is your receipt.

Previous Balance	Charges (+)	Credits (−)	Finance Charge (+)	Account Balance	Amount Now Due

Benn's Department Store
Dayton, Ohio 45410

Payments, returns, and purchases reaching our charge office after billing date will be shown on your next statement.

Please mail or bring saleschecks and credits when making an inquiry on this statement.

4. Do Problem 4 on pages 301 and 302 of your textbook. Write your answers below.

a.

BENN'S DEPARTMENT STORE				
DEPARTMENTAL SALES REPORT				
			WEEK ENDING _____ 19__	
DAY	DEPARTMENTS				TOTAL
TOTALS					

b. _____

c. _____

d. _____

e. _____

f. _____

CHAPTER 11

INVENTORY RECORDS

TOPIC 1 ● LOW-STOCK REPORT Textbook pages 303 to 305

Check Your Reading

Use the spaces below to answer the questions on page 306 of your textbook.

1. _____

_____

2. _____

_____

3. _____

_____

4. _____

5. _____

Exercises for Topic 1

1. Do Exercise 1 on pages 306 to 307 of your textbook. Write your answers in the spaces below and on the form on the next page of your Activity Guide.

   a. _____

_____

_____

_____

_____

_____

_____

   b. Write your answers on the low-stock-report form on the next page of your Activity Guide.

2. Do Exercise 2 on page 307 of your textbook. Write your answers in the spaces below and on the form on the next page of your Activity Guide.

   a. _____

_____

_____

_____

_____

_____

   b. Write your answers on the low-stock-report form on the next page of your Activity Guide.

EXERCISE 1b

LOW STOCK REPORT

Date _____ , 19 ___

Item	Stock No.	Unit	Max-imum	On Hand	Order

EXERCISE 2b

LOW STOCK REPORT

Date _____ , 19 ___

Item	Stock No.	Unit	Max-imum	On Hand	Order

Name _____

Date _____

TOPIC 2 ● STOCK CARDS Textbook pages 308 to 310

Check Your Reading

Use the spaces below to answer the questions on page 310 of your textbook.

1. _____   _____

2. _____   _____

3. _____   _____

4. _____

                                   5. _____

_____

_____

                                   6. _____

_____

Exercises for Topic 2

1. Do Exercise 1 on page 311 of your textbook. Write your answers on the stock cards below and on the next page of your Activity Guide. Save your work for use in Exercises 2 and 3.

STOCK CARD

ITEM			STOCK NO.	
MINIMUM		MAXIMUM		
DATE	NUMBER RECEIVED	NUMBER SOLD	BALANCE	

STOCK CARD

ITEM			STOCK NO.	
MINIMUM		MAXIMUM		
DATE	NUMBER RECEIVED	NUMBER SOLD	BALANCE	

STOCK CARD			
ITEM		STOCK NO.	
MINIMUM		MAXIMUM	
DATE	NUMBER RECEIVED	NUMBER SOLD	BALANCE

STOCK CARD			
ITEM		STOCK NO.	
MINIMUM		MAXIMUM	
DATE	NUMBER RECEIVED	NUMBER SOLD	BALANCE

2. Do Exercise 2 on page 311 of your textbook. Write your answers on the stock cards you prepared in Exercise 1. Save your work for use in Exercise 3.

3. Do Exercise 3 on page 312 of your textbook. Write your answers in the spaces below.

a. _____
_____
_____

b. _____
_____
_____
_____
_____

c. _____

d.

Item	Number Received	Number Sold	Balance
Avanti talking camera	_____	_____	_____
Lens brush	_____	_____	_____
Mixton camera case	_____	_____	_____
Pulsar telephoto lens	_____	_____	_____

24

4. Do Exercise 4 on page 312 of your textbook. Write your answers on the stock cards below and on page 26 of your Activity Guide. Save your work for use in Exercises 5 and 6.

5. Do Exercise 5 on pages 312 to 313 of your textbook. Write your answers on the stock cards you prepared in Exercise 4. Save your work for use in Exercise 6.

EXERCISES 4 AND 5

STOCK CARD

ITEM			STOCK NO.	
MINIMUM		MAXIMUM		
DATE		NUMBER RECEIVED	NUMBER SOLD	BALANCE

STOCK CARD

ITEM			STOCK NO.	
MINIMUM		MAXIMUM		
DATE		NUMBER RECEIVED	NUMBER SOLD	BALANCE

STOCK CARD			
ITEM		STOCK NO.	
MINIMUM		MAXIMUM	
DATE	NUMBER RECEIVED	NUMBER SOLD	BALANCE

STOCK CARD			
ITEM		STOCK NO.	
MINIMUM		MAXIMUM	
DATE	NUMBER RECEIVED	NUMBER SOLD	BALANCE

6. Do Exercise 6 on page 313 of your textbook. Write your answers in the spaces below. Two of the cordless phones that were ordered on December 14 were not received on December 17.

a. _____

_____

_____

b. _____

_____

_____

_____

_____

c. _____

_____

d.

Item	Number Received	Number Sold	Balance
ADX Answerphone	_____	_____	_____
ADX cordless phone	_____	_____	_____
Exeter memory phone	_____	_____	_____
Granby phone/clock radio	_____	_____	_____

Name _____

Date _____

TOPIC 3 ● ORDERING AND RECEIVING STOCK   Textbook pages 313 to 319

Check Your Reading

Use the spaces below to answer the questions on page 320 of your textbook.

1. _____

2. _____

3. _____

4. _____

5. _____

6. _____

7. _____

Exercises for Topic 3

1. Do Exercise 1 on page 320 of your textbook. Write your answers on Purchase Requisition R912 below. Save your work for use in Exercises 3, 5, 7, and 9.

Fashion Phone Center		**PURCHASE REQUISITION**

Date Needed   **Date of Request**   **Requisition No.**

Ship To

Requested By

Quantity		Description
On Hand	**To Order**	

2. Do Exercise 2 on page 321 of your textbook. Write your answers on Purchase Requisition R913 below. Save your work for use in Exercises 4, 6, 8, and 10.

Fashion Phone Center   PURCHASE REQUISITION

Date Needed   **Date of Request**   **Requisition No.**

Ship To

Requested By

On Hand	To Order	Description

(Column group header: **Quantity** over On Hand / To Order)

3. Do Exercise 3 on page 321 of your textbook. Write your answer in the space below.

4. Do Exercise 4 on page 321 of your textbook. Write your answer in the space below.

_____

5. Do Exercise 5 on page 322 of your textbook. Write your answers on Purchase Order 2003 below.

Fashion Phone Center
2378 Glenview Road
Elkins Park, PA 19177

PURCHASE ORDER No. |

TO:

Requisition No.

Date	Items needed by	Terms	Via	

QUANTITY	STOCK NO.	DESCRIPTION	UNIT PRICE	EXTENSION

By _____

Purchasing Agent

RECEIVING COPY

---

6. Do Exercise 6 on page 322 of your textbook. Write your answers on Purchase Order 2004 on page 30 of your Activity Guide.

7. Do Exercise 7 on page 322 of your textbook. Write your answers on Purchase Order 2003, which you prepared above for Exercise 5.

8. Do Exercise 8 on page 322 of your textbook. Write your answers on Purchase Order 2004, which you prepared in Exercise 6, on page 30 of your Activity Guide.

Fashion Phone Center
2378 Glenview Road
Elkins Park, PA 19177

PURCHASE ORDER No.

TO:

Requisition No.

Date	Items needed by	Terms	Via	

QUANTITY	STOCK NO.	DESCRIPTION	UNIT PRICE	EXTENSION

RECEIVING COPY

By _____

Purchasing Agent

---

9. Do Exercise 9 on page 322 of your textbook. Write your answers on the stock card below.

10. Do Exercise 10 on page 322 of your textbook. Write your answers on the stock card below.

EXERCISE 9

STOCK CARD

ITEM Exeter memory phone		STOCK NO. 16-141	
MINIMUM 10		MAXIMUM 20	
DATE	NUMBER RECEIVED	NUMBER SOLD	BALANCE
19— June 1	15		15
3		4	11
6		3	8

EXERCISE 10

STOCK CARD

ITEM ADX Answerphone		STOCK NO. 14-233	
MINIMUM 10		MAXIMUM 40	
DATE	NUMBER RECEIVED	NUMBER SOLD	BALANCE
19— June 1	40		40
4		18	22
6		16	6

Name _____

Date _____

TOPIC 4 ● PERIODIC INVENTORY Textbook pages 323 to 324

Check Your Reading

Use the spaces below to answer the questions on pages 324 to 325 of your textbook.

I. _____

_____

_____

_____

_____

_____

_____

_____

_____

2. _____

_____

_____

3. _____

_____

_____

_____

_____

4. _____

_____

_____

_____

_____

Exercises for Topic 4

I. Do Exercise 1 on page 325 of your textbook. Write your answers on Inventory Sheet 6 on the next page of your Activity Guide.

2. Do Exercise 2 on page 325 of your textbook. Write your answers on Inventory Sheet 4 on the next page of your Activity Guide.

INVENTORY SHEET

Baker Brothers

693 South Street
Boston, MA 01114

Date   Sheet No.

Counted By			Recorded By	Computed By		
STOCK NO.	QUANTITY	UNIT OF COUNT	DESCRIPTION	UNIT PRICE		EXTENSION
				TOTAL		

INVENTORY SHEET

Modern Luggage Inc.

Kahala Mall
Honolulu, HI 96816

Date   Sheet No.

Counted By			Recorded By	Computed By		
STOCK NO.	QUANTITY	UNIT OF COUNT	DESCRIPTION	UNIT PRICE		EXTENSION
				TOTAL		

Name _____

Date _____

END OF CHAPTER ACTIVITIES   Textbook pages 326 to 329

Math Skillbuilder

Do the Math Skillbuilder on page 326 of your textbook. Write any corrections on the stock cards below.

STOCK CARD

NUMBER RECEIVED	NUMBER SOLD	BALANCE
75		75
	12	63
	8	55
	13	42
50		92
	39	53
	13	40
36		76

STOCK CARD

NUMBER RECEIVED	NUMBER SOLD	BALANCE
144		144
	37	107
	26	81
	43	48
72		120
	18	102
	27	75
36		111

Vocabulary Skillbuilder

Do the Vocabulary Skillbuilder on page 327 of your textbook. Use the spaces below to write the term that best matches each statement.

1. _____

2. _____

3. _____

4. _____

5. _____

6. _____

7. _____

8. _____

9. _____

10. _____

Application Problems

1. Do Problem 1 on page 327 of your textbook. Write your answers on the stock cards below and on the next page. Save your work for use in Problems 2 through 8.

STOCK CARD

ITEM			STOCK NO.	
MINIMUM			MAXIMUM	
DATE	NUMBER RECEIVED		NUMBER SOLD	BALANCE

STOCK CARD

ITEM			STOCK NO.	
MINIMUM			MAXIMUM	
DATE	NUMBER RECEIVED		NUMBER SOLD	BALANCE

STOCK CARD

ITEM			STOCK NO.	
MINIMUM			MAXIMUM	

DATE		NUMBER RECEIVED	NUMBER SOLD	BALANCE

STOCK CARD

ITEM			STOCK NO.	
MINIMUM			MAXIMUM	

DATE		NUMBER RECEIVED	NUMBER SOLD	BALANCE

2. Do Problem 2 on pages 327 to 328 of your textbook. Write your answers on the stock cards you prepared in Problem 1 on pages 34 and 35 of this Activity Guide.

3. Do Problem 3 on page 328 of your textbook. Write your answers in the spaces below.

a. _____

b. _____

c. _____

d.

Item	Number Received	Number Sold	Balance
Takeaway steam travel iron	_____	_____	_____
Italia manicure set	_____	_____	_____
Becker shoe shiner	_____	_____	_____
Nocord rotary razor	_____	_____	_____

4. Do Problem 4 on page 328 of your textbook. Write your answers on Purchase Requisition R7073 below.

Cashman's Department Store   PURCHASE REQUISITION

Date Needed   Date of Request   Requisition No.

Ship To

Requested By

Quantity		Description
On Hand	To Order	

5. Do Problem 5 on page 328 of your textbook. Write your answer in the space below.

_____

Date _____

6. Do Problem 6 on page 328 of your textbook. Write your answers on Purchase Order
74630 below.

Cashman's Department Store
814 Grand Avenue • Madison, WI 53704

PURCHASE ORDER No. 74630

TO:

Requisition No.

Date	Items needed by	Terms	Via	
QUANTITY	**STOCK NO.**	**DESCRIPTION**	**UNIT PRICE**	**EXTENSION**

RECEIVING COPY

By _____
Purchasing Agent

7. Do Problem 7 on page 328 of your textbook. Write your answers on the purchase
order you prepared above for Problem 6.

8. Do Problem 8 on page 328 of your textbook. Write your answers on the stock card on the bottom of page 35 of your Activity Guide.

9. Do Problem 9 on pages 328 to 329 of your textbook. Write your answers on the inventory sheet below.

INVENTORY SHEET

Cashman's Department Store
814 Grand Avenue • Madison, WI 53704

Date   Sheet No.   11

Counted By			Recorded By	Computed By			
STOCK NO.	QUANTITY	UNIT OF COUNT	DESCRIPTION	UNIT PRICE		EXTENSION	
			TOTAL				

ACCOUNTS PAYABLE PROCEDURES

TOPIC 1 ● PURCHASE INVOICES   Textbook pages 330 to 332

Check Your Reading

Use the spaces below to answer the questions on page 332 of your textbook.

1. _____   **4.** _____

2. _____   _____

3. _____   **5.** _____

        _____

Exercises for Topic 1

1. Do Exercise 1 on page 333 of your textbook. Write your answers in the spaces below.

a. _____   **b.** _____   **c.** _____   **d.** _____

2. Do Exercise 2 on pages 334 to 335 of your textbook. Write your answers below and on the next page of your Activity Guide. Check each extension and total. If an amount is incorrect, draw a line through it and write the correct amount above it. After you have checked and corrected each, write your initials below the total.

a.

Quantity	Stock No.	Description	Unit Price	Total
6 ea.	5453	Jewel chest	71.00	426.00

c.

Quantity	Stock No.	Description	Unit Price	Total
18 ea.	5050	Wet/dry shaver	26.70	480.60
36 ea.	5076	Shower caddy	7.75	279.00
				659.60

b.

Quantity	Stock No.	Description	Unit Price	Total
30 ea.	6870	Aroma disk player	15.50	465.00
12 ea.	6863	Vanity trio	27.75	333.00
				798.00

d.

Quantity	Stock No.	Description	Unit Price	Total
10 ea.	5665	Oak bookshelf	25.00	250.00
6 ea.	5641	Brass change dish	8.25	49.50
6 ea.	5658	Brass clock	65.25	391.50
				691.00

e.

Quantity	Stock No.	Description	Unit Price	Total
4 ea.	4151	Wool hat	23.65	93.60
12 pr.	9255	Medium wool gloves	8.38	100.56
12 pr.	9256	Large wool gloves	8.38	100.56
				294.72

f.

Quantity	Stock No.	Description	Unit Price	Total
5 sets	9360	Koala golf club covers	11.73	58.65
8 ea.	9318	Golf care kit	7.76	62.08
				120.73

g.

Quantity	Stock No.	Description	Unit Price	Total
15 ea.	5055	Emergency CB	54.77	821.55
25 ea.	8653	Rechargeable flashlight	14.46	316.50
12 ea.	2018	Cordless mini vac	31.20	374.40
6 ea.	2024	Tool and knife set	55.34	332.04
				1,844.49

h.

Quantity	Stock No.	Description	Unit Price	Total
4 ea.	3812	Nordock 450 × telescope	178.75	715.00
2 ea.	3829	Nordock 600 × telescope	276.84	553.68
1 ea.	3820	Nordock reflector telescope	443.90	443.90
				1,722.58

i.

Quantity	Stock No.	Description	Unit Price	Total
9 ea.	6771	Gumball machine	15.49	139.41
12 ea.	5506	Cheese set	12.63	151.56
15 ea.	7245	Wood nutcracker	8.75	131.25
6 ea.	9755	Sleigh with candy	14.88	89.28
				511.50

j.

Quantity	Stock No.	Description	Unit Price	Total
30 ea.	8255	Calligraphy kit	6.32	189.60
24 ea.	8823	Art activity set	8.57	203.28
10 ea.	8802	Wood art chest	12.85	128.50
16 ea.	8800	Crayon case	4.67	74.72
				596.10

Name _____

Date _____

TOPIC 2 ● FINDING DISCOUNTS AND DUE DATES Textbook pages 336 to 337

Check Your Reading

Use the spaces below to answer the questions on page 338 of your textbook.

1. _____

2. _____

3. _____

4. _____

5. _____

Exercises for Topic 2

1. Do Exercise 1 on page 338 of your textbook. Write your answers in the spaces below.

   a. _____   c. _____

   b. _____   d. _____

2. Do Exercise 2 on page 338 of your textbook. Write your answers in the spaces below.

	Due Date of Credit Period	Due Date of Discount Period	Net to Be Paid After Discount
a.	_____	_____	_____
b.	_____	_____	_____
c.	_____	_____	_____
d.	_____	_____	_____
e.	_____	_____	_____
f.	_____	_____	_____
g.	_____	_____	_____
h.	_____	_____	_____
i.	_____	_____	_____
j.	_____	_____	_____
k.	_____	_____	_____
l.	_____	_____	_____
m.	_____	_____	_____

Learning Through Practice

The addition problems below are especially designed to improve your skill in adding 9s, 8s, 7s, 6s, and 5s very rapidly. Add mentally. Do not write down your answers until you are sure you can add each set of problems in the amount of time given.

1. Practice until you can add the two rows in 15 seconds.

8	9	6	7	9	10	5	6	7	8
8	8	6	6	9	9	5	5	7	7

6	6	8	8	5	5	7	7	9	9
6	7	8	9	5	6	7	8	9	10

2. Practice until you can add the two rows in 14 seconds.

7	7	9	9	8	8	5	5	6	6
7	6	9	8	8	7	5	4	6	5

7	6	9	8	8	7	5	4	6	5
7	7	9	9	8	8	5	5	6	6

3. Practice until you can add the two rows in 12 seconds.

7	9	6	8	5	7	4	6	9	11
7	7	6	6	5	5	4	4	9	9

6	6	5	5	7	7	9	9	4	4
6	8	5	7	7	9	9	11	4	6

4. Practice until you can add the two rows in 12 seconds.

8	8	9	9	7	7	6	6	5	5
8	6	9	7	7	5	6	4	5	3

9	7	5	3	8	6	6	4	7	5
9	9	5	5	8	8	6	6	7	7

5. Practice until you can add the two rows in 10 seconds.

6	8	9	7	6	7	8	9	7	7
6	8	9	7	7	9	6	8	8	6

7	3	8	5	5	9	8	6	9	9
5	5	9	7	3	7	7	8	9	8

Name _____

Date _____

TOPIC 3 ● ACCOUNTS PAYABLE PROCEDURES Textbook pages 339 to 343

Check Your Reading

Use the spaces below to answer the questions on page 343 of your textbook.

1. _____

_____

_____

_____

2. _____

3. _____

4. _____

5. a. _____

b. _____

c. _____

Exercises for Topic 3

1. Do Exercise 1 on pages 343 to 344 of your textbook. Write your answers on the creditors' accounts below and on page 44.

Name _____ Account No. _____

Address _____

DATE	EXPLANATION	POST. REF.	DEBIT	CREDIT	BALANCE

Name _____ Account No. _____

Address _____

DATE	EXPLANATION	POST. REF.	DEBIT	CREDIT	BALANCE

Name _____ Account No._____
Address _____

DATE	EXPLANATION	POST. REF.	DEBIT	CREDIT	BALANCE

2. Do Exercise 2 on pages 344 to 345 of your textbook. Write your answers on the creditors' accounts below.

Name _____ Account No._____
Address _____

DATE	EXPLANATION	POST. REF.	DEBIT	CREDIT	BALANCE

Name _____ Account No._____
Address _____

DATE	EXPLANATION	POST. REF.	DEBIT	CREDIT	BALANCE

Name _____ Account No._____
Address _____

DATE	EXPLANATION	POST. REF.	DEBIT	CREDIT	BALANCE

END OF CHAPTER ACTIVITIES Textbook pages 346 to 349

Math Skillbuilder

Do the Math Skillbuilder on page 346 of your textbook. Write your answers in the spaces below.

Discount	Amount to Be Paid		Discount	Amount to Be Paid
a. _____	_____	f. _____		_____
b. _____	_____	g. _____		_____
c. _____	_____	h. _____		_____
d. _____	_____	i. _____		_____
e. _____	_____	j. _____		_____

Vocabulary Skillbuilder

Do the Vocabulary Skillbuilder on pages 346 to 347 of your textbook. In the spaces below, write the term that best matches each statement.

1. _____ 6. _____

2. _____ 7. _____

3. _____ 8. _____

4. _____ 9. _____

5. _____

Application Problems

1. Do Problem 1 on page 347 of your textbook. Write your answers on the creditors' account forms on page 46 of your Activity Guide. Save your work for use in Problem 3.

2. Do Problem 2 on pages 347 to 349 of your textbook. Write your answers on the invoices on pages 47 and 48 of your Activity Guide. Check each extension and total. If an amount is incorrect, draw a line through it and write the correct amount above it. After you have checked and corrected each invoice, write your initials in the lower-right corner of each invoice. Save your work for use in Problem 3.

Name _____ Account No._____

Address _____

DATE	EXPLANATION	POST. REF.	DEBIT	CREDIT	BALANCE

Name _____ Account No._____

Address _____

DATE	EXPLANATION	POST. REF.	DEBIT	CREDIT	BALANCE

3. Do Problem 3 on page 349 of your textbook. Write your answers on the creditors' account forms you prepared above for Problem 1. In the Date column, enter the date of the invoice. Write the creditor's account number on each of the invoices checked in Problem 2 after the invoice has been posted.

4. Do Problem 4 on page 349 of your textbook. Write your answers in the spaces below.

Invoice Number	a. Due Date of the Credit Period	b. Due Date of the Discount Period	c. Amount to Be Paid After Discount
11719	_____	_____	_____
793414	_____	_____	_____
11990	_____	_____	_____
793606	_____	_____	_____
12194	_____	_____	_____
794045	_____	_____	_____

PROBLEM 2

Goldberg & Dell
❊ Fashions ❊

INVOICE NO.
11719

INVOICE DATE Sept. 2, 19--

TERMS 2/10, n/30

QUANTITY	STOCK NO.	DESCRIPTION	UNIT PRICE	AMOUNT
2 doz.	114-8	Sweater vest	234.75	469.50
4 doz.	127-2	Crew socks	26.40	105.60
			Total	575.10

Sunshine Apparel Manufacturers

INVOICE NO.
793414

INVOICE DATE Sept. 7, 19--

TERMS 1/10, n/60

QUANTITY	STOCK NO.	DESCRIPTION	UNIT PRICE	AMOUNT
38	29-1441	Unlined jacket	48.75	1,852.50
45	29-1466	Silk dress	84.79	3,815.55
9	32-2002	Fur-trimmed coat	260.00	2,340.00
			Total	8,008.15

Goldberg & Dell
❊ Fashions ❊

INVOICE NO.
11990

INVOICE DATE Sept. 16, 19--

TERMS 2/10, n/30

QUANTITY	STOCK NO.	DESCRIPTION	UNIT PRICE	AMOUNT
124	138-02	Prewashed jeans	17.63	2,186.12
85	167-41	Wool slacks	38.27	3,252.95
60	143-81	Western shirt	28.40	1,704.00
18	147-20	Linen suit	118.45	2,133.72
			Total	9,276.79

PROBLEM 2 *(continued)*

Sunshine Apparel Manufacturers

INVOICE NO.
793606

INVOICE DATE Sept. 21, 19--

TERMS 1/10, n/60

QUANTITY	STOCK NO.	DESCRIPTION	UNIT PRICE	AMOUNT
2 doz.	23-4118	Running suit	186.55	373.10
75	26-0615	Cotton blouse	21.12	1,584.00
24	14-1701	Corduroy jumper	48.00	1,152.00
40	32-2018	Leather jacket	83.25	3,330.00
			Total	6,439.10

Goldberg & Dell
❧ Fashions ❧

INVOICE NO.
12194

INVOICE DATE Sept. 30, 19--

TERMS 2/10, n/30

QUANTITY	STOCK NO.	DESCRIPTION	UNIT PRICE	AMOUNT
4 doz.	127-4	Ski sweater	372.45	1,489.80
65	163-8	Skirt and top	75.00	4,875.00
6	181-1	All-weather coat	143.75	862.50
			Total	7,227.30

Sunshine Apparel Manufacturers

INVOICE NO.
794045

INVOICE DATE Sept. 30, 19--

TERMS 1/10, n/60

QUANTITY	STOCK NO.	DESCRIPTION	UNIT PRICE	AMOUNT
12 doz.	20-1478	Knit pullover	151.63	1,819.65
30 doz.	20-1526	Printed T-shirt	62.52	1,867.50
			Total	3,687.15

CHAPTER 13

PAYROLL RECORDS

TOPIC 1 ● COMPUTING TIME AND EARNINGS Textbook pages 350 to 357

Check Your Reading

Use the spaces below to answer the questions on page 357 of your textbook.

1. _____   _____

   _____

   _____   3. _____

   _____   _____

   _____   _____

2. _____   4. _____

   _____   5. _____

Exercises for Topic 1

1. Do Exercise 1 on pages 357 to 359 of your textbook. Write your answers on the time cards below and on the next page of your Activity Guide.

Helping Hint: See pages 351 to 352 and 353 to 356 of your textbook for information about computing hours worked and about recording weekly earnings.

a.

Week Ending				April 29, 19 --		
No. 499-21-7645						
Name Burks, A. R.						

Days	Regular				Overtime		Daily Totals
	In	Out	In	Out	In	Out	
Mon.	8^{25}	12^{05}	1^{05}	4^{35}			
Tues.	8^{15}	12^{10}	1^{00}	4^{30}			
Wed.	8^{20}	12^{05}	1^{00}	4^{25}			
Thurs.	8^{10}	12^{05}	1^{05}	4^{45}			
Fri.	8^{15}	12^{05}	1^{05}	4^{45}			
Sat.							
Sun.							

		Hours	Rate	Earnings
	Regular		8.30	
	Overtime			
Days Worked	Total Hours		Gross Earnings	

b.

Week Ending				April 29, 19 --		
No. 528-91-4924						
Name Galdos, N.						

Days	Regular				Overtime		Daily Totals
	In	Out	In	Out	In	Out	
Mon.	8^{00}	12^{00}	1^{00}	4^{30}			
Tues.	8^{15}	12^{00}	1^{00}	4^{30}			
Wed.	8^{30}	12^{00}	1^{45}	4^{40}			
Thurs.	8^{15}	11^{55}	1^{00}	4^{45}			
Fri.	8^{20}	12^{00}	12^{55}	4^{30}			
Sat.							
Sun.							

		Hours	Rate	Earnings
	Regular		8.90	
	Overtime			
Days Worked	Total Hours		Gross Earnings	

c.

Week Ending				April 29, 19 --		
No. 354-12-2033						
Name Liebert, G. H.						

Days	Regular				Overtime		Daily Totals
	In	Out	In	Out	In	Out	
Mon.	8³⁵	12³⁰	1⁰⁰	4⁰⁰			
Tues.	8²⁵	12²⁵	1⁰⁰	4⁰⁵			
Wed.	8²⁵	12³⁰	1⁰⁰	4²⁵			
Thurs.	8³⁰	12³⁰	1⁰⁵	4⁰⁰			
Fri.	8³⁵	12³⁵	1⁰⁰	4¹⁵			
Sat.							
Sun.							

		Hours	Rate	Earnings
	Regular		6.70	
	Overtime			
Days Worked	Total Hours		Gross Earnings	

d.

Week Ending				April 29, 19 --		
No. 634-34-7066						
Name Ponczka, E. E.						

Days	Regular				Overtime		Daily Totals
	In	Out	In	Out	In	Out	
Mon.	8³⁵	11³⁵	12⁰⁵	4⁴⁰			
Tues.	8³⁰	11³⁰	12⁰⁰	4⁴⁰			
Wed.	8²⁵	11³⁰	12⁰⁰	4⁴⁵			
Thurs.	8⁰⁰	11³⁰	11⁵⁵	4³⁰			
Fri.	8³⁰	11³⁵	12⁰⁰	4²⁵			
Sat.							
Sun.							

		Hours	Rate	Earnings
	Regular		9.10	
	Overtime			
Days Worked	Total Hours		Gross Earnings	

e.

Week Ending				April 29, 19 --		
No. 649-51-1101						
Name Sotos, W. G.						

Days	Regular				Overtime		Daily Totals
	In	Out	In	Out	In	Out	
Mon.	7²⁵	12⁰⁵	1⁰⁵	4⁰⁵			
Tues.	7⁴⁵	11³⁰	1⁰⁰	4⁴⁰			
Wed.	7³⁰	11⁵⁰	12⁵⁵	4²⁰			
Thurs.	8²⁰	12¹⁰	1¹⁰	4²⁵			
Fri.	7³⁰	11¹⁵	12⁵⁰	3⁴⁵			
Sat.							
Sun.							

		Hours	Rate	Earnings
	Regular		10.00	
	Overtime			
Days Worked	Total Hours		Gross Earnings	

f.

Week Ending				April 29, 19 --		
No. 397-55-6814						
Name Yung, C.						

Days	Regular				Overtime		Daily Totals
	In	Out	In	Out	In	Out	
Mon.	7³⁵	12⁰⁰	1¹⁰	4³⁵			
Tues.	7²⁰	12⁰⁰	12⁵⁵	4¹⁵			
Wed.	7²⁵	11²⁵	1⁰⁵	4²⁵			
Thurs.	7³⁵	11⁵⁵	12⁵⁰	4⁰⁵			
Fri.	7⁴⁰	11³⁰	12⁵⁵	4²⁵			
Sat.							
Sun.							

		Hours	Rate	Earnings
	Regular		9.90	
	Overtime			
Days Worked	Total Hours		Gross Earnings	

Name _____

Date _____

2. Do Exercise 2 on page 359 of your textbook. Write your answers on the payroll earnings record below.

DJR COMPANY	PAYROLL EARNINGS RECORD							
	For the week ended _____ 19 _____							
EMPLOYEE NUMBER	NAME	REGULAR HOURS	REGULAR RATE	REGULAR EARNINGS	OVERTIME HOURS	OVERTIME RATE	OVERTIME EARNINGS	GROSS EARNINGS

3. Do Exercise 3 on pages 359 to 360 of your textbook. Write your answers on the payroll earnings record below.

LYONS COMPANY	PAYROLL EARNINGS RECORD							
	For the week ended _____ 19 _____							
EMPLOYEE NUMBER	NAME	REGULAR HOURS	REGULAR RATE	REGULAR EARNINGS	OVERTIME HOURS	OVERTIME RATE	OVERTIME EARNINGS	GROSS EARNINGS

4. Do Exercise 4 on page 360 of your textbook. Write your answers on the payroll earnings record below.

KRON COMPANY									

PAYROLL EARNINGS RECORD

For the week ended _____ 19 _____

EMPLOYEE NUMBER	NAME	REGULAR HOURS	REGULAR RATE	REGULAR EARNINGS	OVERTIME HOURS	OVERTIME RATE	OVERTIME EARNINGS	GROSS EARNINGS

Name _____

Date _____

TOPIC 2 ● PIECEWORK   Textbook pages 360 to 361

Check Your Reading

Use the spaces below to answer the questions on page 362 of your textbook.

1. _____

_____

_____

2. _____

_____

_____

_____

_____

_____

_____

_____

_____

Exercises for Topic 2

1. Do Exercise 1 on page 362 of your textbook. Compute the total pieces and total weekly earnings on a straight piece rate basis for the following employees. The piecework rate is $1.50 per unit each day.

	Name	Mon.	Tues.	Wed.	Thurs.	Fri.	Total Pieces	Total Weekly Earnings
a.	Abdel, A. H.	41	38	34	40	39	_____	_____
b.	Goldmann, P. H.	32	31	29	30	36	_____	_____
c.	Lewis, R. L.	33	31	30	35	34	_____	_____
d.	Pettus, A. G.	29	29	30	32	29	_____	_____
e.	Trotti, B.	25	23	25	24	26	_____	_____
f.	Wilson, D. C.	40	41	44	40	43	_____	_____
g.	Yee, G. Y.	43	46	46	45	48	_____	_____
h.	Zirkle, W. D.	31	34	34	36	38	_____	_____

2. Do Exercise 2 on page 362 of your textbook. Compute the total pieces and total weekly earnings on a straight piece rate basis for the following employees. Each employee's rate is listed.

Name	Mon.	Tues.	Wed.	Thurs.	Fri.	Daily Piecework Rate	Total Pieces	Total Weekly Earnings
a. Abrams, D. L.	183	176	191	160	181	$0.28	_____	_____
b. Cook, A. G.	329	343	354	318	366	0.16	_____	_____
c. Dunn, R.	389	384	371	401	396	0.20	_____	_____
d. Esposito, K. J.	399	412	436	421	419	0.12	_____	_____
e. Farr, W. O.	1,208	1,183	1,306	1,422	1,215	0.04	_____	_____
f. Paulz, D. D.	218	193	240	220	310	0.24	_____	_____
g. Sutphin, A. L.	398	413	382	461	393	0.23	_____	_____
h. Terry, M. S.	512	496	483	501	491	0.15	_____	_____

3. Do Exercise 3 on page 363 of your textbook. Compute the total weekly earnings on a differential piece rate basis for the following employees. Use the differential piece rate scale shown below.

Units per Day	Daily Rate per Unit
First 40	$0.75
Next 20	1.00
Over 60	1.25

Name	Mon.	Tues.	Wed.	Thurs.	Fri.	Total Weekly Earnings
a. Bilinski, J.	43	51	48	55	54	_____
b. Guthrie, R. W.	54	60	58	52	59	_____
c. Lyons, V. S.	67	63	63	65	64	_____
d. Pumo, M. A.	45	43	48	49	51	_____
e. Schultz, D. L.	34	39	38	36	33	_____
f. Syzman, T.	61	58	54	60	62	_____

TOPIC 3 ● COMMISSION WAGES Textbook pages 363 to 364

Check Your Reading

Use the spaces below to answer the questions on page 365 of your textbook.

1. _____

2. _____

3. _____
_____
_____
_____
_____
_____
_____

Exercises for Topic 3

1. Do Exercise 1 on page 365 of your textbook. Using the daily sales totals below, compute total sales and total commission on a straight-commission basis for these salespeople. The commission rate is 10 percent.

	Employee	Mon.	Tues.	Wed.	Thurs.	Fri.	Sat.	Total Sales	Total Commission
a.	Biddix, L.	$468.37	—	$621.89	—	$1,121.10	$ 556.80	_____	_____
b.	Dang, C. V.	554.18	$676.21	—	$741.19	801.01	667.12	_____	_____
c.	Harris, M.	667.44	512.21	807.32	350.00	—	834.40	_____	_____
d.	Meli, A. P.	392.81	—	900.50	476.37	805.61	—	_____	_____
e.	Simko, G.	530.07	392.24	676.91	—	1,107.09	—	_____	_____
f.	Worsham, P.	—	699.80	—	963.21	1,226.81	1,463.11	_____	_____

2. Do Exercise 2 on page 365 of your textbook. Using the weekly sales totals below, compute the total commission on a straight-commission basis for these salespeople. The commission rate is 3 percent.

	Employee	Total Weekly Sales	Total Commission
a.	Baldini, L. G.	$28,627.50	_____
b.	Carrico, M. A.	17,126.85	_____
c.	Haq, N.	33,662.27	_____
d.	Pappin, B. R.	8,919.60	_____
e.	Tuzzo, R. M.	14,895.05	_____
f.	Wright, J. W.	23,091.24	_____

3. Do Exercise 3 on pages 365 to 366 of your textbook. Using the daily sales totals below, compute (1) total hourly wages, (2) total sales, (3) total commission, and (4) total weekly earnings on a wage-plus-commission basis for each of these sales-people. Each employee worked 40 hours for the week. The commission rate is 6 percent.

Employee	Mon.	Tues.	Wed.	Thurs.	Fri.	Hourly Wage	Total Hourly Wages	Total Sales	Total Commission	Total Weekly Earnings
a. Bolstein, L. W.	$243.18	$231.12	$300.70	$256.01	$196.21	$5.25				
b. Davis, C.	219.18	246.87	224.43	272.11	242.31	6.00				
c. Huber, T. A.	304.76	220.20	218.76	212.66	344.77	5.75				
d. McMunn, A. G.	289.19	196.86	248.94	314.11	256.40	4.75				
e. Owen, A. B.	200.18	401.11	506.62	298.42	117.12	6.25				
f. Siff, W. R.	308.20	94.38	321.12	341.17	230.00	5.00				

Name _____

Date _____

END OF CHAPTER ACTIVITIES   Textbook pages 367 to 372

Math Skillbuilder

Do the Math Skillbuilder for figuring the total hours worked on page 367 of your textbook. Use the spaces below to write your answers.

1. _____   6. _____

2. _____   7. _____

3. _____   8. _____

4. _____   9. _____

5. _____   10. _____

Do the Math Skillbuilder for computing pay at time and a half on pages 367 to 368 of your textbook. Use the spaces below to write your answers.

	Overtime Hours	Hourly Rate	Overtime Rate	Time-and-a-Half Pay
1.	10	$ 8.00	_____	_____
2.	5	9.00	_____	_____
3.	10	11.10	_____	_____
4.	8	10.30	_____	_____
5.	4.5	9.00	_____	_____
6.	2	8.40	_____	_____
7.	4	7.30	_____	_____
8.	12	8.20	_____	_____
9.	15	15.80	_____	_____
10.	3	6.83	_____	_____

Vocabulary Skillbuilder

Do the Vocabulary Skillbuilder on page 368 of your textbook. Use the spaces below to write the term that best matches each statement.

1. _____   6. _____

2. _____   7. _____

3. _____   8. _____

4. _____   9. _____

5. _____   10. _____

Application Problems

1. Do Problem 1 on page 369 of your textbook. Write your answers below.

Week Ending				January 9, 19 --		
No. 573-12-9874						
Name Holdren, W. T.						

Days	Regular				Overtime		Daily Totals
	In	Out	In	Out	In	Out	
Mon.	8³⁰	12⁰⁰	1⁰⁰	4³⁰			
Tues.	8³⁰	12⁰⁰	1¹⁰	4⁴⁰			
Wed.	8²⁵	12⁰⁰	1⁰⁰	5⁴⁵			
Thurs.	8³⁵	12⁰⁵	1⁰⁵	4³⁰			
Fri.	8³⁰	12⁰⁵	1⁰⁰	4⁴⁰			
Sat.							
Sun.							

		Hours	Rate	Earnings
	Regular		8.40	
	Overtime			
Days Worked	Total Hours		Gross Earnings	

Week Ending				January 9, 19 --		
No. 589-33-0562						
Name Santos, G. K.						

Days	Regular				Overtime		Daily Totals
	In	Out	In	Out	In	Out	
Mon.	8³⁰	12⁰⁰	1⁰⁰	5³⁰			
Tues.	8²⁵	12⁰⁰	1⁰⁵	4⁴⁰			
Wed.	8³⁰	12⁰⁰	1⁰⁵	4⁴⁰			
Thurs.	8³⁰	12⁰⁰	1⁰⁵	4³⁵			
Fri.	8²⁰	12⁰⁰	1⁰⁰	4⁴⁵			
Sat.							
Sun.							

		Hours	Rate	Earnings
	Regular		10.15	
	Overtime			
Days Worked	Total Hours		Gross Earnings	

2. Do Problem 2 on page 369 of your textbook. Write your answers on the time cards below and on the next page.

Week Ending				July 22, 19 --		
No. 493-80-5297						
Name Burks, A. D.						

Days	Regular				Overtime		Daily Totals
	In	Out	In	Out	In	Out	
Mon.	8⁰⁰	12⁰²	1⁰⁰	6⁰⁰			
Tues.	7⁵⁵	12⁰¹	12⁵⁶	7⁰⁰			
Wed.	7⁵⁰	12⁰⁰	12⁵⁸	7³⁰			
Thurs.	8⁰⁰	12⁰⁴	1⁰²	6³⁰			
Fri.	7⁵⁸	12⁰⁵	12⁵⁹	5⁰⁰			
Sat.	7⁵⁹	12⁰⁰					
Sun.							

		Hours	Rate	Earnings
	Regular		10.20	
	Overtime			
Days Worked	Total Hours		Gross Earnings	

Week Ending				July 22, 19 --		
No. 534-66-4392						
Name Cueno, A. C.						

Days	Regular				Overtime		Daily Totals
	In	Out	In	Out	In	Out	
Mon.	7⁵⁰	12⁰²	1⁰⁰	7³⁰			
Tues.	8⁰⁰	12⁰⁰	12⁵⁴	6⁰⁰			
Wed.	7⁵²	12⁰²	12⁵⁸	7⁰⁰			
Thurs.	7⁵⁸	12⁰⁵	12⁵⁹	6³⁰			
Fri.	8⁰⁰	12⁰³	12⁵⁷	5⁰⁰			
Sat.	7⁵⁶	12⁰⁰					
Sun.							

		Hours	Rate	Earnings
	Regular		7.90	
	Overtime			
Days Worked	Total Hours		Gross Earnings	

Date _____

PROBLEM 2 *(continued)*

Week Ending	July 22, 19 --

No. 587-20-2986

Name Happel, R. C.

Days	Regular				Overtime		Daily Totals
	In	Out	In	Out	In	Out	
Mon.	8^{20}	12^{00}	1^{00}	5^{30}			
Tues.	8^{04}	12^{03}	1^{02}	6^{00}			
Wed.	8^{10}	12^{01}	1^{01}	5^{00}			
Thurs.	8^{00}	12^{00}	1^{00}	6^{30}			
Fri.	8^{02}	12^{03}	1^{02}	5^{00}			
Sat.							
Sun.							
			Hours	Rate	Earnings		
		Regular		11.00			
		Overtime					
Days Worked		Total Hours		Gross Earnings			

Week Ending	July 22, 19 --

No. 652-87-3433

Name Lau, H. H.

Days	Regular				Overtime		Daily Totals
	In	Out	In	Out	In	Out	
Mon.	9^{00}	12^{05}	1^{02}	6^{00}			
Tues.	9^{10}	12^{02}	1^{00}	5^{00}			
Wed.	7^{55}	12^{00}	12^{55}	4^{00}			
Thurs.	7^{58}	12^{03}	12^{59}	5^{30}			
Fri.	7^{59}	12^{00}	12^{52}	5^{00}			
Sat.	8^{00}	12^{05}					
Sun.							
			Hours	Rate	Earnings		
		Regular		9.80			
		Overtime					
Days Worked		Total Hours		Gross Earnings			

Week Ending	July 22, 19 --

No. 329-86-7910

Name Alonso, H.

Days	Regular				Overtime		Daily Totals
	In	Out	In	Out	In	Out	
Mon.	8^{00}	12^{05}	1^{00}	5^{04}			
Tues.	7^{57}	12^{00}	12^{58}	3^{00}			
Wed.	8^{40}	12^{03}	12^{55}	6^{00}			
Thurs.	7^{59}	12^{07}	1^{02}	7^{30}			
Fri.	8^{02}	12^{01}	12^{52}	6^{30}			
Sat.							
Sun.							
			Hours	Rate	Earnings		
		Regular		9.60			
		Overtime					
Days Worked		Total Hours		Gross Earnings			

Week Ending	July 22, 19 --

No. 358-99-0002

Name Bess, C. F.

Days	Regular				Overtime		Daily Totals
	In	Out	In	Out	In	Out	
Mon.	7^{55}	12^{00}	1^{02}	5^{00}			
Tues.	9^{00}	12^{05}	12^{53}	5^{02}			
Wed.	8^{30}	12^{03}	12^{58}	5^{04}			
Thurs.	8^{00}	12^{01}	12^{56}	7^{30}			
Fri.	7^{50}	12^{04}	12^{57}	6^{30}			
Sat.	8^{00}	12^{00}					
Sun.							
			Hours	Rate	Earnings		
		Regular		8.80			
		Overtime					
Days Worked		Total Hours		Gross Earnings			

3. Do Problem 3 on pages 369 to 371 of your textbook. Write your answers on the payroll earnings record below. List the names of the employees in alphabetical order.

CONWAY AND FREEMAN

PAYROLL EARNINGS RECORD

For the week ended _____ 19 _____

EMPLOYEE NUMBER	NAME	REGULAR HOURS	REGULAR RATE	REGULAR EARNINGS	OVERTIME HOURS	OVERTIME RATE	OVERTIME EARNINGS	GROSS EARNINGS

4. Do Problem 4 on page 371 of your textbook. Write your answers on the payroll earnings record below.

CYCLE COMPANY

PAYROLL EARNINGS RECORD

For the week ended _____ 19 _____

EMPLOYEE NUMBER	NAME	REGULAR HOURS	REGULAR RATE	REGULAR EARNINGS	OVERTIME HOURS	OVERTIME RATE	OVERTIME EARNINGS	GROSS EARNINGS

60

5. Do Problem 5 on page 372 of your textbook. Compute the total weekly earnings on a differential piece rate basis for the following employees. Use the differential piece rate scale given on page 372 of your textbook.

	Employee	Mon.	Tues.	Wed.	Thurs.	Fri.	Total Weekly Earnings
a.	Arjona, J. D.	14	16	15	17	15	_____
b.	Crostic, A. C.	17	18	16	15	17	_____
c.	Hughes, J. W.	21	20	19	19	20	_____
d.	Melfi, J.	13	16	14	12	17	_____
e.	Scouras, C. M.	19	20	18	19	21	_____
f.	Yun, H. H.	22	18	19	21	18	_____

6. Do Problem 6 on page 372 of your textbook. Using the weekly sales totals below, compute (1) total hourly wages, (2) total commission, and (3) total weekly earnings on a wage-plus-commission basis for each of these salespeople. Each employee worked 35 hours for the week. The commission rate is 5 percent.

	Employee	Weekly Sales	Hourly Wage	Total Hourly Wages	Total Commission	Weekly Earnings
a.	Askew, W. W.	$8,126.18	$7.50	_____	_____	_____
b.	Campanello, A. S.	8,728.05	6.75	_____	_____	_____
c.	Davis, C.	6,314.44	7.50	_____	_____	_____
d.	Gratz, C.	7,079.52	7.00	_____	_____	_____
e.	Hiltz, L. H.	6,364.59	6.75	_____	_____	_____
f.	Link, G. R.	8,419.06	7.50	_____	_____	_____

Learning Through Practice

1. As an employee of Brady Manufacturing Company, part of your job involves verifying pairs of figures. Verify the following by placing a check mark (✔) beside those pairs that are alike and an X beside those that are different.

a. ___563194	563914		**j.** ___1093275	1903275
b. ___830791	830791		**k.** ___3675283	3675283
c. ___877312	877132		**l.** ___3942775	3942775
d. ___101932	101923		**m.** ___8392549	8932549
e. ___758630	758630		**n.** ___4234876	4234876
f. ___426189	426819		**o.** ___5893334	5893334
g. ___697335	697335		**p.** ___6118287	6111828
h. ___322186	322186		**q.** ___7428543	7428543
i. ___524934	524349		**r.** ___2122622	2126622

2. Brady pays its salespeople 6 percent commission on all sales, plus another 2 percent on all sales over $15,000 per month. Sheila Boyd sold $25,000 worth of merchandise this month. How much money should she receive as her total pay?

_____

3. Brad Wilson also works at the Brady Manufacturing Company. Brad sold $23,500 worth of merchandise this month. How much money should he receive as his total pay?

_____

4. Assume that you are going to read some invoice totals to a coworker. Write the words you will use to read the following amounts of money. Try to express the figures in as few words as possible. The first one is done for you.

   a. $1,005 <u>One thousand five dollars</u>_____

   b. $16,003 _____

   c. $555.88 _____

   d. $818.88 _____

   e. $15,215.16 _____

   f. $800.44 _____

   g. $333.69 _____

   h. $24,467.28 _____

CHAPTER 14

TAX RECORDS AND PAYROLL REPORTS

TOPIC 1 ● SOCIAL SECURITY TAX AND MEDICARE TAX   Textbook pages 373 to 378

Check Your Reading

Use the spaces below to answer the questions on page 377 of your textbook.

1. _____
2. _____
   _____
3. _____
4. _____
   _____
5. _____
6. _____
7. _____
   _____
8. _____

Exercises for Topic 1

1. Do Exercise 1 on page 377 in your textbook. Write your answers below

Soc. Sec. Tax	Medicare Tax	Employee + Employer Contribution
a.		
b.		
c.		
d.		
e.		
f.		

2. Do Exercise 2 on page 378 in your textbook. Write your answers below.

   a. _____
   b. _____
   c. _____
   d. _____
   e. _____

3. Do Exercise 3 on page 378 of your textbook. Write your answers below.

Social
Security Tax | Medicare Tax

a. _____ _____

b. _____ _____

c. _____ _____

d. _____ _____

e. _____ _____

f. _____ _____

g. _____ _____

h. _____ _____

i. _____ _____

j. _____ _____

4. Do Exercise 4 on page 378 of your textbook. Write your answers below.

Gross Annual
Earnings | Annual Social
Security Tax | Annual
Medicare Tax

a. _____ _____ _____

b. _____ _____ _____

c. _____ _____ _____

d. _____ _____ _____

e. _____ _____ _____

f. _____ _____ _____

Name _____

Date _____

Topic 2 ● Federal Income Taxes   Textbook pages 378 to 382.

Check Your Reading

Use the spaces below to answer the questions on page 380 to 381 of your textbook.

1. _____
   _____
   _____
   _____
   _____
   _____
   _____

2. _____

3. _____
   _____
   _____
   _____
   _____
   _____

4. _____
   _____
   _____
   _____
   _____
   _____

5. _____
   _____
   _____
   _____
   _____

Exercises for Topic 2

1. Do Exercise 1 on page 382 of your textbook. Write your answers below.

   a. _____
   b. _____
   c. _____
   d. _____

2. Do Exercise 2 on page 382 of your textbook. Write your answers below.

	Soc. Sec. Tax	Medicare Tax	Federal Income Tax	Total Taxes and Additional Deduction	Net Pay
a.	_____	_____	_____	_____	_____
b.	_____	_____	_____	_____	_____
c.	_____	_____	_____	_____	_____
d.	_____	_____	_____	_____	_____
e.	_____	_____	_____	_____	_____
f.	_____	_____	_____	_____	_____
g.	_____	_____	_____	_____	_____

Name _____

Date _____

TOPIC 3 ● THE PAYROLL REGISTER AND OTHER DEDUCTIONS   Textbook pages 382 to 386

Check Your Reading

Use the spaces below to answer the questions on page 385 of your textbook.

1. _____
_____
_____
_____

2. _____
_____
_____
_____

3. _____
_____
_____
_____
_____

4. _____
_____
_____
_____
_____
_____

5. _____
_____
_____
_____
_____

6. _____
_____
_____
_____
_____

Exercises for Topic 3

1. Do Exercise 1 on page 385 of your textbook. Write your answers on the Deductions section of the register below.

DEDUCTIONS						
FEDERAL INCOME TAX	SOC. SEC. TAX	MEDI-CARE TAX	INSUR-ANCE	OTHER		TOTAL
17 00	14 65	3 41	22 90	20 00		
22 00	17 88	4 16	23 80	30 00		
15 00	15 71	3 65	22 90			
16 00	12 66	2 94	23 80			
14 00	11 02	2 56	22 90	20 00		
13 00	12 36	2 87	23 80	25 00		
18 00	16 21	3 77	23 80	30 00		
21 00	17 62	4 10	23 80	20 00		

2. Do Exercise 2 on page 385 of your textbook. Write your answers on the Deductions section of the register above.

3. Do Exercise 3 on page 386 of your textbook. Write your answers on the payroll register shown below.

LANTERN OUTBACK CO.

PAYROLL REGISTER

For the Week Beginning May 5, 19__ And Ending May 9, 19__ Paid May 16, 19__

EMPLOYEE DATA					EARNINGS			DEDUCTIONS						NET PAY	
EMPLOYEE NUMBER	NAME	MAR. STATUS	ALLOW-ANCES	HRS	REGULAR	OVERTIME	TOTAL	FEDERAL INCOME TAX	SOC. SEC. TAX	MEDI-CARE TAX	INSUR-ANCE	OTHER	TOTAL	AMOUNT	CH. NO.
598-23-9613	Aeckerle, Sally	S	0	40	490 00		490 00	75 00	30 38	7 11					
469-11-2855	Berkowitz, John	S	1	48	600 00	180 00	780 00	143 00	48 36	11 31					
466-81-3740	Field, Martha	m	2	39	598 65		598 65	59 00	37 12	8 68					
520-13-5386	Harmon, Robert	S	1	40	448 00		448 00	53 00	27 78	6 50					
487-92-6779	Kipler, Andrew	S	1	40	500 00		500 00	65 00	31 00	7 25					
432-76-1268	LaMont, Richard	S	2	40	640 00		640 00	92 00	39 68	9 28					
464-31-3062	Smith, Jane	m	3	42	632 00	47 40	679 40	64 00	42 12	9 85					
549-46-5511	Whipple, Kenneth	M	2	40	652 00		652 00	68 00	40 42	9 45					

4. Do Exercise 4 on page 386 of your textbook. Write your answers on the payroll register shown below.

SNIDER ENTERPRISES

PAYROLL REGISTER

For the Week Beginning ———— 19 —— And Ending ———— 19 —— Paid ———— 19 ——

EMPLOYEE DATA				EARNINGS			DEDUCTIONS						NET PAY	
EMPLOYEE NUMBER	NAME	MAR. STATUS	ALLOW- ANCES	HRS										
				REGULAR	OVERTIME	TOTAL	FEDEAL INCOME TAX	SOC. SEC. TAX	MEDI- CARE TAX	INSUR- ANCE	OTHER	TOTAL	AMOUNT	CH. NO.

70

Name _____

Date _____

TOPIC 4 ● PAYCHECKS, EARNINGS RECORDS, AND TAX STATEMENTS   Textbook pages 387 to 393

Check Your Reading

Use the spaces below to answer the questions on page 392 of your textbook.

1. _____
_____
_____

2. _____
_____
_____

3. _____
_____
_____

4. _____
_____
_____

5. _____
_____

6. _____
_____
_____

7. _____
_____

8. _____
_____
_____

9. _____
_____
_____

Exercises for Topic 4

1. Use the following payroll register for the week ending January 15 to complete Exercise 1.

NORTHERN COMPANY

PAYROLL REGISTER

For the Week Beginning January 8, 19___ And Ending January 15, 19___ Paid January 20, 19___

| EMPLOYEE DATA | | | | | EARNINGS | | | DEDUCTIONS | | | | | | NET PAY | |
EMPLOYEE NUMBER	NAME	MAR. STATUS	ALLOW-ANCES	HRS	REGULAR	OVERTIME	TOTAL	FEDEAL INCOME TAX	SOC. SEC. TAX	MEDI-CARE TAX	INSUR-ANCE	OTHER	TOTAL	AMOUNT	CH. NO.
569-98-1405	Decker, Richard K.	M	4	45	440 00	82 50	522 50	35 00	32 40	7 58	16 90	5 00	96 88	425 62	
542-13-2001	Harris, Marlena P.	S	1	42	440 00	33 00	473 00	58 00	29 33	6 86	14 40	5 00	113 59	359 41	
499-18-8124	Wilson, Elaine A.	M	2	40	408 00	— —	408 00	30 00	25 30	5 92	16 90	5 00	83 12	324 88	

72

Name _____

Date _____

a. Do Exercise 1a on page 392 of your textbook. Write your answers on the checks below.

		Regular	Overtime	Total	Income Tax	Soc. Sec. Tax	Medicare Tax	Insurance	Other	Total	Amount	Ch. No.
Period Ending	Hours Worked		Earnings					Deductions				Net Pay

Employee Pay Statement
Detach and retain for your records

Northern Company
Fargo, ND

- -

Northern Company
344 Summit Drive
Fargo, ND 43781-0216

PAYROLL
CHECK   NO. _____ $\frac{82\text{-}21}{640}$

_____ 19 ___

Pay To
The Order of _____ $ _____

_____ Dollars

ROCK OF TRUST BANK
FARGO, ND 43781-0346

_____

		Regular	Overtime	Total	Income Tax	Soc. Sec. Tax	Medicare Tax	Insurance	Other	Total	Amount	Ch. No.
Period Ending	Hours Worked		Earnings					Deductions				Net Pay

Employee Pay Statement
Detach and retain for your records

Northern Company
Fargo, ND

- -

Northern Company
344 Summit Drive
Fargo, ND 43781-0216

PAYROLL
CHECK   NO. _____ $\frac{82\text{-}21}{640}$

_____ 19 ___

Pay To
The Order of _____ $ _____

_____ Dollars

ROCK OF TRUST BANK
FARGO, ND 43781-0346

_____

(continued)

		Regular	Overtime	Total	Income Tax	Soc. Sec. Tax	Medicare Tax	Insurance	Other	Total	Amount	Ch. No.
Period Ending	Hours Worked	Earnings			Deductions						Net Pay	

Employee Pay Statement
Detach and retain for your records

Northern Company
Fargo, ND

- -

Northern Company
344 Summit Drive
Fargo, ND 43781-0216

PAYROLL
CHECK   NO. _____   82-21 / 640

_____ 19 ___

Pay To
The Order of _____ $ _____

_____ Dollars

ROCK OF TRUST BANK
FARGO, ND 43781-0346

_____

EXERCISE 1 (continued)

b. Do Exercise 1b on page 392 of your textbook. Write your answers on the employee earnings records below and on page 76.

EMPLOYEE EARNINGS RECORD FOR YEAR 19——

Name *Decker, Richard K.* Social Security No. *568-98-1405*

Address *19 East Avenue* Marital Status *M*

Casselton, ND 43762-0381 Withholding Allowances *4*

Phone *(413) 555-5690* Position *Small Parts Mechanic*

Date of Birth *June 4, 1964* Date Employed *August 23, 19——*

PAY PERIOD ENDING	RATE PER HOUR	HRS	EARNINGS REGULAR	OVERTIME	TOTAL	DEDUCTIONS FEDERAL INCOME TAX	SOC. SEC. TAX	MEDI-CARE TAX	INSUR-ANCE	OTHER	TOTAL	NET PAY	YEAR-TO-DATE EARNINGS
1/1/--	11 00	43	440 00	49 50	489 50	29 00	30 35	7 10	16 90	5 00	88 35	401 15	489 50
1/8/--	11 00	40	440 00		440 00	23 00	27 28	6 38	16 90	5 00	78 56	361 44	929 50

EMPLOYEE EARNINGS RECORD FOR YEAR 19——

Name *Harris, Marlena P.* Social Security No. *542-13-2001*

Address *241 Park Street* Marital Status *S*

Fargo, ND 43783-2204 Withholding Allowances *1*

Phone *(413) 555-1089* Position *Programmer*

Date of Birth *May 5, 1961* Date Employed *April 29, 19——*

PAY PERIOD ENDING	RATE PER HOUR	HRS	EARNINGS REGULAR	OVERTIME	TOTAL	DEDUCTIONS FEDERAL INCOME TAX	SOC. SEC. TAX	MEDI-CARE TAX	INSUR-ANCE	OTHER	TOTAL	NET PAY	YEAR-TO-DATE EARNINGS
1/1/--	11 00	38	418 00		418 00	49 00	25 92	6 06	14 40	5 00	100 38	317 62	418 00
1/8/--	11 00	40	440 00		440 00	53 00	27 28	6 38	14 40	5 00	106 06	333 94	858 00

(continued)

EMPLOYEE EARNINGS RECORD FOR YEAR 19--

Name _Wilson, Elaine A._

Address _1074 Sturgis Road_

Casselton, ND 43762-1985

Phone _(413) 555-1895_

Date of Birth _January 23, 1960_

Social Security No. _499-18-8124_

Marital Status _M_

Withholding Allowances _2_

Position _Sales Associate_

Date Employed _June 9, 19--_

PAY PERIOD ENDING	RATE PER HOUR	HRS	EARNINGS			DEDUCTIONS							NET PAY	YEAR-TO-DATE EARNINGS
			REGULAR	OVERTIME	TOTAL	FEDERAL INCOME TAX	SOC. SEC. TAX	MEDI-CARE TAX	INSUR-ANCE	OTHER	TOTAL			
1/1/--	10 20	40	408 00		408 00	30 00	25 30	5 92	16 90	5 00	83 12	324 88	408 00	
1/8/--	10 20	41	408 00	15 30	423 30	33 00	26 24	6 14	16 90	5 00	87 28	336 02	831 30	

2. Do Exercise 2 on page 392 of your textbook. Write your answers on the three Form W-2 below and on page 78.

1 Control number	22222	For Official Use Only ▶ OMB No. 1545-0008					
2 Employer's name, address, and ZIP code			**6** Statutory employee ☐ Deceased ☐ Pension plan ☐ Legal rep. ☐ 942 emp. ☐ Subtotal ☐ Deferred compensation ☐ Void ☐				
			7 Allocated tips			8 Advance EIC payment	
			9 Federal income tax withheld			10 Wages, tips, other compensation	
3 Employer's identification number		4 Employer's state I.D. number	11 Social security tax withheld			12 Social security wages	
5 Employee's social security number			13 Social security tips			14 Medicare wages and tips	
19a Employee's name (first, middle initial, last)			15 Medicare tax withheld			16 Nonqualified plans	
			17 See Instrs. for Form W-2			18 Other	
19b Employee's address and ZIP code							
20		21	22 Dependent care benefits			23 Benefits included in Box 10	
24 State income tax	25 State wages, tips, etc.	26 Name of state	27 Local income tax		28 Local wages, tips, etc.		29 Name of locality

Copy A For Social Security Administration   Department of the Treasury—Internal Revenue Service

Form **W-2 Wage and Tax Statement 1992**   13-2581759

(continued)

1 Control number		22222	For Official Use Only ▶ OMB No. 1545-0008					
2 Employer's name, address, and ZIP code			6 Statutory employee ☐	Deceased ☐	Pension plan ☐	Legal rep. ☐	942 emp. ☐	Subtotal ☐ Deferred compensation ☐	Void ☐
			7 Allocated tips				8 Advance EIC payment	
			9 Federal income tax withheld				10 Wages, tips, other compensation	
3 Employer's identification number	4 Employer's state I.D. number		11 Social security tax withheld				12 Social security wages	
5 Employee's social security number			13 Social security tips				14 Medicare wages and tips	
19a Employee's name (first, middle initial, last)			15 Medicare tax withheld				16 Nonqualified plans	
			17 See Instrs. for Form W-2				18 Other	
19b Employee's address and ZIP code								
20	21		22 Dependent care benefits				23 Benefits included in Box 10	
24 State income tax	25 State wages, tips, etc.	26 Name of state	27 Local income tax		28 Local wages, tips, etc.		29 Name of locality	

Copy A For Social Security Administration Department of the Treasury—Internal Revenue Service

Form **W-2 Wage and Tax Statement 1992** 13-2581759

1 Control number		22222	For Official Use Only ▶ OMB No. 1545-0008					
2 Employer's name, address, and ZIP code			6 Statutory employee ☐	Deceased ☐	Pension plan ☐	Legal rep. ☐	942 emp. ☐	Subtotal ☐ Deferred compensation ☐	Void ☐
			7 Allocated tips				8 Advance EIC payment	
			9 Federal income tax withheld				10 Wages, tips, other compensation	
3 Employer's identification number	4 Employer's state I.D. number		11 Social security tax withheld				12 Social security wages	
5 Employee's social security number			13 Social security tips				14 Medicare wages and tips	
19a Employee's name (first, middle initial, last)			15 Medicare tax withheld				16 Nonqualified plans	
			17 See Instrs. for Form W-2				18 Other	
19b Employee's address and ZIP code								
20	21		22 Dependent care benefits				23 Benefits included in Box 10	
24 State income tax	25 State wages, tips, etc.	26 Name of state	27 Local income tax		28 Local wages, tips, etc.		29 Name of locality	

Copy A For Social Security Administration Department of the Treasury—Internal Revenue Service

Form **W-2 Wage and Tax Statement 1992** 13-2581759

3. Use the following payroll register for the week ending March 29 to complete Exercise 3.

COMPU-CENTER COMPANY

PAYROLL REGISTER

For the Week Beginning March 25, 19 — — And Ending March 29, 19 — — Paid April 5, 19 — —

| EMPLOYEE DATA | | | | | EARNINGS | | | DEDUCTIONS | | | | | | NET PAY | |
EMPLOYEE NUMBER	NAME	MAR. STATUS	ALLOW-ANCES	HRS	REGULAR	OVERTIME	TOTAL	FEDEAL INCOME TAX	SOC. SEC. TAX	MEDI-CARE TAX	INSUR-ANCE	OTHER	TOTAL	AMOUNT	CH. NO.
532-69-1808	Akera, Dennis C.	M	3	40	650 00		650 00	61 00	40 30	9 43	13 50	10 00	134 23	515 77	
591-26-3481	Fernandez, Rita A.	M	2	42	600 00	45 00	645 00	66 00	39 99	9 35	12 50		127 84	517 16	
563-91-2114	Kim, Sung Y.	S	1	40	610 00		610 00	96 00	37 82	8 85	13 50	5 00	161 17	448 83	
414-83-2297	Sousa, Calvin R.	S	0	48	520 00	156 00	676 00	125 00	41 91	9 80	13 50	5 00	195 21	480 79	
					2,380 00	201 00	2,581 00	348 00	160 02	37 43	53 00	20 00	618 45	1,962 55	

EXERCISE 3

(continued)

a. Do Exercise 3a on page 393 of your textbook. Write your answers on the payroll check below and the payroll register on the previous page.

		Regular	Overtime	Total	Income Tax	Soc. Sec. Tax	Medicare Tax	Insurance	Other	Total	Amount	Ch. No.
Period Ending	Hours Worked		Earnings				Deductions					Net Pay

Employee Pay Statement
Detach and retain for your records

Compu-Center Company
Dallas, TX

– –

Compu-Center Company
1892 Fairfax Drive
Dallas, TX 75207-8499

PAYROLL
CHECK   NO. _____   82-21
                                              640

_____ 19 ____

Pay To
The Order of _____ $ _____

_____ Dollars

TEXAS STAR BANK
DALLAS, TX 75216-7056

_____

EXERCISE 3

(continued)

b. Do Exercise 3b on page 393 of your textbook. Write your answers on the employee's earnings record shown below.

EMPLOYEE EARNINGS RECORD FOR YEAR 19__

Name *Akers, Dennis C.*

Address *21 South Gate Road*

Dallas, TX 75217-3625

Phone *(270) 555-8269*

Date of Birth *May 10, 1963*

Social Security No. *532-69-1808*

Marital Status *M*

Withholding Allowances *3*

Position *Jr. Systems Analyst*

Date Employed *December 14, 19--*

PAY PERIOD ENDING	RATE PER HOUR	HRS	EARNINGS REGULAR	EARNINGS OVERTIME	EARNINGS TOTAL	FEDERAL INCOME TAX	SOC. SEC. TAX	MEDI-CARE TAX	INSUR-ANCE	OTHER	TOTAL	NET PAY	YEAR-TO-DATE EARNINGS
1/4/--	16 25	40	650 00		650 00	61 00	40 30	9 43	13 50	10 00	134 23	515 77	650 00
1/11/--	16 25	40	650 00		650 00	61 00	40 30	9 43	13 50	10 00	134 23	515 77	1,300 00
1/18/--	16 25	40	650 00		650 00	61 00	40 30	9 43	13 50	10 00	134 23	515 77	1,950 00
1/25/--	16 25	40	650 00		650 00	61 00	40 30	9 43	13 50	10 00	134 23	515 77	2,600 00
2/1/--	16 25	40	650 00		650 00	61 00	40 30	9 43	13 50	10 00	134 23	515 77	3,250 00
2/8/--	16 25	43	650 00	73 14	723 14	72 00	44 83	10 49	13 50	10 00	150 82	572 32	3,973 14
2/15/--	16 25	41	650 00	24 38	674 38	64 00	41 81	9 78	13 50	10 00	139 09	535 29	4,647 52
2/22/--	16 25	45	650 00	121 90	771 90	79 00	47 86	11 19	13 50	10 00	161 55	610 35	5,419 42
3/1/--	16 25	40	650 00		650 00	61 00	40 30	9 43	13 50	10 00	134 23	515 77	6,069 42
3/8/--	16 25	40	650 00		650 00	61 00	40 30	9 43	13 50	10 00	134 23	515 77	6,719 42
3/15/--	16 25	40	650 00		650 00	61 00	40 30	9 43	13 50	10 00	134 23	515 77	7,369 42
3/22/--	16 25	40	650 00		650 00	61 00	40 30	9 43	13 50	10 00	134 23	515 77	8,019 42
QUARTERLY TOTALS													

(continued)

c. Do Exercise 3c on page 393 of your textbook. Write your answers on the employee's earnings record shown on page 81 of your Activity Guide.

d. Do Exercise 3d on page 393 of your textbook. Write your answers on Form W-2 below.

1 Control number ⬛⬛⬛ **22222**	**For Official Use Only ▶** OMB No. 1545-0008	

2 Employer's name, address, and ZIP code	**6** Statutory employee ☐ Deceased ☐ Pension plan ☐ Legal rep. ☐ 942 emp. ☐ Subtotal ☐ Deferred compensation ☐ Void ☐

	7 Allocated tips	**8** Advance EIC payment
	9 Federal income tax withheld	**10** Wages, tips, other compensation

3 Employer's identification number	**4** Employer's state I.D. number	**11** Social security tax withheld	**12** Social security wages
5 Employee's social security number		**13** Social security tips	**14** Medicare wages and tips

19a Employee's name (first, middle initial, last)	**15** Medicare tax withheld	**16** Nonqualified plans
	17 See Instrs. for Form W-2	**18** Other

19b Employee's address and ZIP code

20	**21**	**22** Dependent care benefits	**23** Benefits included in Box 10

24 State income tax	**25** State wages, tips, etc.	**26** Name of state	**27** Local income tax	**28** Local wages, tips, etc.	**29** Name of locality

Copy A For Social Security Administration   Department of the Treasury—Internal Revenue Service

Form **W-2 Wage and Tax Statement 1992**   13-2581759

Name _____

Date _____

END OF CHAPTER ACTIVITIES   Textbook pages 394 to 397

Math Skillbuilder

Do the Math Skillbuilder for rounding to the nearest cent on page 394 of your text-book. Write your answers in the spaces below.

1. _____   6. _____
2. _____   7. _____
3. _____   8. _____
4. _____   9. _____
5. _____   10. _____

Do the Math Skillbuilder for computing social security and Medicare taxes on page 394 of your textbook. Write your answers below.

1. _____   6. _____
2. _____   7. _____
3. _____   8. _____
4. _____   9. _____
5. _____   10. _____

Vocabulary Skillbuilder

Do the Vocabulary Skillbuilder on page 395 of your textbook. Use the spaces below to write the term that best matches each statement.

1. _____
2. _____
3. _____
4. _____
5. _____
6. _____
7. _____
8. _____
9. _____
10. _____

Application Problems

1. Do Problem 1 on pages 395 to 396 of your textbook. Write your answers on the payroll register shown on page 85 of your Activity Guide.

2. Do Problem 2 on pages 396 to 397 of your textbook. Write your answers on the employee's earning record, and Form W-2 on page 86 in your Activity Guide.

Exploring Computers in Recordkeeping
Textbook pages 397 to 399

Check Your Reading

1. _____

_____

2. _____

_____

3. _____

_____

4. _____

_____

_____

_____

5. _____

_____

_____

_____

PROBLEM I

Do Problem 1 on pages 395 to 396 of your textbook. Write your answers on the payroll register shown below.

Note: Round off overtime earnings, social security, and Medicare deductions, but do not round off overtime rates. Calculate social security tax at 6.2% and Medicare tax at 1.45%.

KWAN LEE ORIENTAL IMPORTS

PAYROLL REGISTER

For the Week Beginning _____ 19 ___ And Ending _____ 19 ___ Paid _____ 19 ___ _____ 19 ___

EMPLOYEE DATA					EARNINGS			DEDUCTIONS					NET PAY	
EMPLOYEE NUMBER	NAME	MAR. STATUS	ALLOW-ANCES	HRS	REGULAR	OVERTIME	TOTAL	FEDERAL INCOME TAX	SOC. SEC. TAX	MEDI-CARE TAX	INSUR-ANCE	OTHER	TOTAL	AMOUNT	CK. NO.

PROBLEM 2

EMPLOYEE EARNINGS RECORD FOR YEAR 19____

Name _____   Social Security No. _____

Address _____   Marital Status _____

_____   Withholding Allowances _____

Phone _____   Position _____

Date of Birth _____   Date Employed _____

PAY PERIOD ENDING	RATE PER HOUR	HRS	EARNINGS			DEDUCTIONS						NET PAY	YEAR-TO-DATE EARNINGS
			REGULAR	OVERTIME	TOTAL	FEDERAL INCOME TAX	SOC. SEC. TAX	MEDI-CARE TAX	INSUR-ANCE	OTHER	TOTAL		
10/8/--		43											
10/15/--		40											
10/22/--		40											
10/29/--		46											
11/5/--		42											
11/12/--		40											
11/19/--		39											
11/26/--		40											
12/3/--		43											
12/10/--		41											
12/17/--		40											
12/24/--		40											
12/31/--		40											
QUARTERLY TOTALS													

1 Control number	22222	For Official Use Only ▶ OMB No. 1545-0008		

2 Employer's name, address, and ZIP code	6 Statutory employee ☐ Deceased ☐ Pension plan ☐ Legal rep. ☐ 942 emp. ☐ Subtotal ☐ Deferred compensation ☐ Void ☐
	7 Allocated tips	8 Advance EIC payment
	9 Federal income tax withheld	10 Wages, tips, other compensation

3 Employer's identification number	4 Employer's state I.D. number	11 Social security tax withheld	12 Social security wages

5 Employee's social security number	13 Social security tips	14 Medicare wages and tips

19a Employee's name (first, middle initial, last)	15 Medicare tax withheld	16 Nonqualified plans
	17 See Instrs. for Form W-2	18 Other

19b   Employee's address and ZIP code

20	21	22 Dependent care benefits	23 Benefits included in Box 10

24 State income tax	25 State wages, tips, etc.	26 Name of state	27 Local income tax	28 Local wages, tips, etc.	29 Name of locality

Copy A For Social Security Administration   Department of the Treasury—Internal Revenue Service

Form **W-2 Wage and Tax Statement 1992**   13-2581759

86

PROJECT 3
SHOES FOR SPORTS

Textbook pages 400 to 404

Complete the project that appears on pages 400 to 404 of your textbook. Use the forms below and on pages 87 to 92 of your Activity Guide.

Name _____ Account No._____
Address _____

DATE	EXPLANATION	DEBIT	CREDIT	BALANCE

Name _____ Account No._____
Address _____

DATE	EXPLANATION	DEBIT	CREDIT	BALANCE

Name _____ Account No._____
Address _____

DATE	EXPLANATION	DEBIT	CREDIT	BALANCE

STOCK CARD

ITEM			STOCK NO.
MINIMUM		MAXIMUM	

DATE		NUMBER RECEIVED	NUMBER SOLD	BALANCE

STOCK CARD

ITEM			STOCK NO.
MINIMUM		MAXIMUM	

DATE		NUMBER RECEIVED	NUMBER SOLD	BALANCE

STOCK CARD

ITEM			STOCK NO.
MINIMUM		MAXIMUM	

DATE		NUMBER RECEIVED	NUMBER SOLD	BALANCE

STOCK CARD

ITEM			STOCK NO.
MINIMUM		MAXIMUM	

DATE		NUMBER RECEIVED	NUMBER SOLD	BALANCE

PROJECT 3 ● SHOES FOR SPORTS

Name _____

Date _____

Name _____ Account No._____
Address _____

DATE		EXPLANATION	DEBIT	CREDIT	BALANCE

Name _____ Account No._____
Address _____

DATE		EXPLANATION	DEBIT	CREDIT	BALANCE

Name _____ Account No._____
Address _____

DATE		EXPLANATION	DEBIT	CREDIT	BALANCE

Name _____ Account No._____
Address _____

DATE		EXPLANATION	DEBIT	CREDIT	BALANCE

Name _____ Account No._____

Address _____

DATE	EXPLANATION	DEBIT	CREDIT	BALANCE

Name _____ Account No._____

Address _____

DATE	EXPLANATION	DEBIT	CREDIT	BALANCE

Name _____

Date _____

Card 1

Week Ending _____ June 28, 19 --

No. 176-27-9091

Name Burge, Rolf

Days	Regular				Overtime		Daily Totals
	In	Out	In	Out	In	Out	
Mon.	7^{55}	11^{05}	12^{55}	5^{00}			
Tues.	7^{55}	12^{00}	1^{00}	4^{55}			
Wed.	8^{00}	12^{00}	12^{55}	5^{00}			
Thurs.	7^{55}	11^{55}	1^{00}	4^{55}			
Fri.	8^{00}	12^{05}	1^{05}	5^{05}			
Sat.							
Sun.							

		Hours	Rate	Earnings
	Regular		10.50	
	Overtime			
Days Worked	Total Hours		Gross Earnings	

Card 2

Week Ending _____ June 28, 19 --

No. 302-14-5918

Name McMinnis, Sarah

Days	Regular				Overtime		Daily Totals
	In	Out	In	Out	In	Out	
Mon.	7^{55}	12^{00}	1^{00}	5^{00}			
Tues.	8^{00}	12^{05}	12^{55}	5^{05}			
Wed.	7^{55}	11^{55}	1^{05}	5^{00}	6^{00}	9^{00}	
Thurs.	7^{55}	12^{05}	1^{00}	5^{05}	6^{05}	9^{05}	
Fri.	8^{05}	12^{00}	12^{55}	4^{55}			
Sat.							
Sun.							

		Hours	Rate	Earnings
	Regular		9.75	
	Overtime			
Days Worked	Total Hours		Gross Earnings	

Card 3

Week Ending _____ June 28, 19 --

No. 414-76-6012

Name Melesco, Naomi

Days	Regular				Overtime		Daily Totals
	In	Out	In	Out	In	Out	
Mon.	7^{55}	12^{05}	12^{55}	5^{00}			
Tues.	8^{45}	12^{00}	1^{00}	5^{05}			
Wed.	8^{00}	12^{05}	1^{05}	4^{55}			
Thurs.	8^{00}	11^{55}	12^{55}	4^{55}			
Fri.	8^{00}	11^{55}	12^{55}	5^{05}			
Sat.							
Sun.							

		Hours	Rate	Earnings
	Regular		11.00	
	Overtime			
Days Worked	Total Hours		Gross Earnings	

Card 4

Week Ending _____ June 28, 19 --

No. 321-40-1799

Name Sanchez, Raoul

Days	Regular				Overtime		Daily Totals
	In	Out	In	Out	In	Out	
Mon.	8^{05}	11^{55}	1^{05}	5^{05}			
Tues.	8^{00}	12^{00}	1^{00}	5^{00}			
Wed.	8^{00}	12^{00}	12^{55}	4^{55}	6^{00}	9^{05}	
Thurs.	8^{05}	11^{55}	12^{55}	4^{05}			
Fri.	8^{05}	12^{05}	12^{55}	5^{00}			
Sat.							
Sun.							

		Hours	Rate	Earnings
	Regular		9.85	
	Overtime			
Days Worked	Total Hours		Gross Earnings	

SHOES FOR SPORTS

PAYROLL REGISTER

For the Week Beginning _____ 19 ___ And Ending _____ 19 ___ Paid _____ 19 ___ _____ 19 ___

EMPLOYEE DATA					EARNINGS			DEDUCTIONS						NET PAY	
EMPLOYEE NUMBER	NAME	MAR. STATUS	ALLOW- ANCES	HRS	REGULAR	OVERTIME	TOTAL	FEDEAL INCOME TAX	SOC. SEC. TAX	MEDI- CARE TAX	INSUR- ANCE	OTHER	TOTAL	AMOUNT	CH. NO.

CHAPTER 15

INTRODUCTION TO ACCOUNTING

TOPIC 1 ◆ ASSETS, LIABILITIES, AND OWNER'S EQUITY
Textbook pages 406 to 412

Check Your Reading

Use the spaces below to answer the questions on page 412 of your textbook.

1. _____
2. _____
3. _____
4. _____
5. a. _____
   b. _____
   c. _____
6. _____
7. _____
8. _____
9. _____
   _____
   _____
10. _____

Exercises for Topic 1

1. Do Exercise 1 on page 413 of your textbook. Write your answers in the Owner's Equity column.

Assets	= Liabilities +	Owner's Equity
a. $95,000 =	$8,000 +	_____
b. $23,546 =	$9,346 +	_____
c. $22,500 =	$3,350 +	_____
d. $31,250 =	$8,708 +	_____
e. $18,435 =	$6,345 +	_____
f. $9,605 =	$1,205 +	_____
g. $45,349 =	$9,728 +	_____
h. $20,090 =	$5,900 +	_____

2. Do Exercise 2 on page 413 of your textbook. Answer below.

Helping Hint: Use the balance sheet on page 407 of your textbook as a model. Remember that the assets are not totaled until the right side of the balance sheet is finished.

Check Your Work: Is the heading centered at the top of the balance sheet? Does it give the name of the business, the title of the statement, and the date? If your answer to any of the above questions is no, correct your work.

3. Do Exercise 3 on page 413 of your textbook. Answer below.

4. Do Exercise 4 on page 413 of your textbook. Write your answers below.

Helping Hint: Use the balance sheet on page 409 of your textbook as a model. Remember that you do not total the assets until the right side of the balance sheet is completed. (You will complete the right side of a balance sheet when you do Exercise 5.)

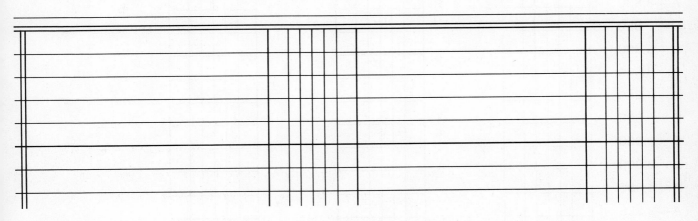

5. Do Exercise 5 on page 413 of your textbook. Write your answers below.

Helping Hint: Now that you are completing the right side of the balance sheet, total the Assets section.

Check Your Work: Does the total of the right side equal the total of the left side? _____ If the totals are not equal, locate your error or errors.

Learning Through Practice

Look at the form below. Write all the A amounts under *Assets,* all the L amounts under *Liabilities,* and all the O amounts under *Owner's Equity.* The first two are done for you. When you have recorded all the amounts, total each of the three columns.

	Assets	=	Liabilities	+	Owner's Equity
L— 3,480			3 4 8 0 00		
O—2,220					2 2 2 0 00
A—8,830					
O— 850					
L— 5,890					
L— 3,560					
A—7,245					
O— 565					
O—5,320					
L— 2,000					
A—4,980					
A—2,328					
O—4,543					
L— 870					
A—8,415					
L— 3,900					
O—1,100					
A—2,500					
TOTALS					

Check Your Work: Add the total of the Liabilities column to the total of the Owner's Equity column. The sum of the totals of these two columns should be the same as the total of the Assets column.

TOPIC 2 ◆ ACCOUNTS   Textbook pages 414 to 416

Check Your Reading

Use the spaces below to answer the questions on page 417 of your textbook.

_____

2. _____

3. _____

_____

4. _____

_____

5. a.

 b. _____

6. a.

 b. _____

7. _____

8. _____

9. _____

Exercises for Topic 2

1. Do Exercise 1 on page 417 of your textbook.

Helping Hint: See pages 415 to 416 of your textbook for information about opening an account.

    a. Write your answers to Exercise 1a on the forms below. The first one is done for you as an example.

Cash

$3,000.00

    b. Answer Exercise 1b below.

Debits	=	**Credits**
Total _____	=	Total _____

Check Your Work: Do the total debits equal the total credits? _____ If they do not agree, locate your error or errors.

2. Do Exercise 2 on page 418 of your textbook.

    a. Write your answers to Exercise 72 on the forms below.

Name _____

Date _____

b. Answer Exercise 2b below.

Debits	=	**Credits**
_____		_____
_____		_____
_____		_____
Total _____	=	Total _____

Check Your Work: Do the total debits equal the total credits? _____ If the total debits and credits do not agree, locate your error or errors.

3. Do Exercise 3 on page 418 of your textbook.

a. Write your answers to Exercise 3a below.

Debits	=	**Credits**
_____		_____
_____		_____
_____		_____
Total _____	=	Total _____

b. Answer Exercise 3b on the form below.

Learning Through Practice

Look at the T accounts below. Use the space next to each account to answer the following questions: (a) Which side (debit or credit) is larger? (b) How much larger? The first answer has been filled in as an example.

1.

Cash	
$2,640.00	$600.10
776.50	58.75
2,327.94	

Total debits = $5,744.44

Total credits = $658.85

2.

Thomas Post, Capital	
$1,229.63	$4,506.73
2,472.36	8,774.27
	38,837.16

Total debits = _____

Total credits = _____

3.

Mortgage Payable	
$861.55	$94,812.27
429.73	5,624.18
	6,507.33

Total debits = _____

Total credits = _____

Name _____

Date _____

TOPIC 3 ◆ CHANGES IN ACCOUNTS Textbook pages 419 to 425

Check Your Reading

Use the spaces below to answer the questions on page 425 of your textbook.

1. a. _____   d. _____

   b. _____   e. _____

   c. _____   f. _____

2. _____

3. _____

_____

_____

_____

_____

4. _____

_____

5. _____

_____

_____

Exercises for Topic 3

1. Do Exercise 1 on page 425 of your textbook. Write your answers on the form below.

Helping Hint: Review pages 419 to 420 of your textbook for information about recording increases and decreases in assets.

2. Do Exercise 2 on page 425 of your textbook. Write your answers on the form below.

Check Your Work: Did you record increases on the debit side and decreases on the credit side? If you did not, correct your work.

3. Do Exercise 3 on page 426 of your textbook. Write your answers on the form below.

```
_____|_____
_____|_____
_____|_____
                        |
```

4. Do Exercise 4 on page 426 of your textbook.

Helping Hint: See pages 420 to 421 of your textbook for information about trans-actions involving two assets.

a.–c. Write your answers for Exercises 4a, 4b, and 4c on the forms below.

```
_____|_____        _____|_____
_____|_____        _____|_____
_____|_____        _____|_____
            |                                |
```

d. Write your answers for Exercise 4d in the spaces below.

Cash on hand after the purchase: _____

Total cost of the furniture on hand: _____

5. Do Exercise 5 on page 426 of your textbook. Answer below.

Helping Hint: See pages 421 to 422 of your textbook.

```
_____|_____
_____|_____
_____|_____
                        |
```

Check Your Work: Did you remember to record the original liability on the credit side of the account? Did you record the increase on the credit side and the decrease on the debit side? If you made any errors, correct your work.

6. Do Exercise 6 on page 426 of your textbook. Answer below.

```
_____|_____        _____|_____
_____|_____        _____|_____
_____|_____        _____|_____
            |                                |

_____|_____        _____|_____
_____|_____        _____|_____
_____|_____        _____|_____
            |                                |
```

7. Do Exercise 7 on page 426 of your textbook. Answer below.

Helping Hint: See pages 423 to 424 of your textbook for a review of where increases in owner's equity and decreases in owner's equity are recorded on the owner's equity account.

8. Do Exercise 8 on page 427 of your textbook. Write your answers on the forms below.

Note: Save your work for use in Exercise 4 of Topic 4 in this chapter.

Learning Through Practice

1. Listed below are the names of six accounts, each one followed by a transaction that affected the account. Use the blanks to write whether each account was increased or decreased and whether the account should be debited or credited. The first one is done for you as an example.

Account	Transaction	Increased or Decreased	Debited or Credited
a. Car	Bought a car.	Increased	Debited
b. Truck	Sold a truck.	_____	_____
c. Cash	Paid electric bill.	_____	_____
d. Cash	Received money from a customer.	_____	_____
e. Accts. Rec./ Customer	Received money from a customer on account.	_____	_____
f. Office Furniture	Sold old office desk.	_____	_____

2. Complete the following accounting equations by filling in the missing figures.

	Assets	= Liabilities + Owner's Equity
a.	_____	= $5,690 + $12,500
b.	_____	= $25,982 + $72,350
c.	_____	= $3,500 + $9,860
d.	_____	= $2,900 + $8,350
e.	_____	= $5,840 + $13,456
f.	_____	= $9,850 + $20,650
g.	_____	= $1,545 + $6,750
h.	_____	= $11,100 + $43,925
i.	_____	= $7,650 + $17,890

3. Look at the liability account shown below. Four amounts are recorded on the account. On the lines next to the account, write which amounts are increases and which are decreases.

Notes Payable	
$400	$810
250	300

Increases _____

Decreases _____

Name _____

Date _____

TOPIC 4 ◆ ACCOUNT BALANCES Textbook pages 427 to 429

Check Your Reading

Use the spaces below to answer the questions on pages 429 to 430 of your textbook.

1. _____

2. _____

3. _____

4. _____

Exercises for Topic 4

1. Do Exercise 1 on page 430 of your textbook. Answer below.

Helping Hint: Use the T account for cash on page 429 of your textbook as a model.

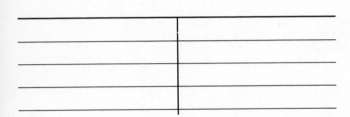

2. Do Exercise 2 on page 430 of your textbook. Answer below.

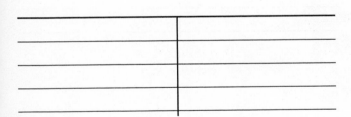

3. Do Exercise 3 on pages 430 to 431 of your textbook.

   a. Write your answers to Exercise 3a on the forms below.

(blank accounting forms)

   b. Answer Exercise 3b below.

	Debits	=		Credits
Total _____		=	Total _____	

Check Your Work: Are the total debit balances and the total credit balances equal? _____ If not, locate your error or errors.

Name _____

Date _____

4. Do Exercise 4 on page 431 of your textbook.

    a. Write your answers for Exercise 4a on the accounts that you prepared in Exercise 8 on page 97 of this Activity Guide.

    b. Answer 4b below.

Debits	=	**Credits**
_____		_____
_____		_____
_____		_____
_____		_____
Total _____	=	Total _____

    Are the total debit balances and the total credit balances equal? _____

5. Do Exercise 5 on pages 431 to 432 of your textbook.

Helping Hint: Work tables are classified as equipment in this business.

    a.–c. Write your answers for Exercises 5a, 5b, and 5c on the forms below.

d. Answer Exercise 5d in the spaces below.

Debits	=	Credits
_____		_____
_____		_____
_____		_____
_____		
Total _____	=	Total _____

Are the total debit balances and total credit balances equal? _____

6. Do Exercise 6 on page 432 of your textbook.

a.–c. Write your answers to Exercises 6a, 6b, and 6c on the forms below.

d. Answer Exercise 6d in the spaces below.

Debits	=	Credits
_____		_____
_____		_____
_____		_____
Total _____	=	Total _____

Are the total debit balances and the total credit balances equal? _____

END OF CHAPTER ACTIVITIES Textbook pages 433 to 437

Math Skillbuilder

Do the Math Skillbuilder on page 433 of your textbook. Write your answers in the spaces below.

1. _____ 2. _____ 3. _____ 4. _____

Vocabulary Skillbuilder

Do the Vocabulary Skillbuilder on pages 433 to 434 of your textbook. Use the spaces below to write the term that best matches each statement.

1. _____	11. _____	21. _____
2. _____	12. _____	22. _____
3. _____	13. _____	23. _____
4. _____	14. _____	24. _____
5. _____	15. _____	25. _____
6. _____	16. _____	26. _____
7. _____	17. _____	27. _____
8. _____	18. _____	28. _____
9. _____	19. _____	29. _____
10. _____	20. _____	

Application Problems

1. Do Problem 1 on page 435 of your textbook. Write the correct term (*asset, liability,* or *owner's equity*) in the spaces below.

   a. _____   d. _____   g. _____

   b. _____   e. _____   h. _____

   c. _____   f. _____

2. Do Problem 2 on page 435 of your textbook. Write your answers in the spaces below.

   a. _____   b. _____   c. _____

3. Do Problem 3 on page 435 of your textbook. Prepare your balance sheet on the form below.

4. Do Problem 4 on page 435 of your textbook. Write your answer on the form below.

5. Do Problem 5 on page 435 of your textbook. Use the space next to each account to answer the following questions: (1) Which side (debit or credit) is larger? (2) How much larger? The first answer has been filled in as an example.

a.

Cash	
$500.00	$50.00

(1) Debit _____

(2) $450.00 _____

b.

Accts. Rec./Bing Company	
$996.20	$445.23

(1) _____

(2) _____

c.

Equipment	
$14,945.00	$945.80

(1) _____

(2) _____

d.

Car	
$7,940.50	

(1) _____

(2) _____

e.

Accts. Pay./R. M. Crandall	
$98.51	$920.43

(1) _____

(2) _____

f.

Monique Hunt, Capital	
$4,980.50	$12,000.00

(1) _____

(2) _____

g.

Furniture	
$4,423.00	$918.20

(1) _____

(2) _____

h.

Accts. Pay./Joanne Nash	
$33.88	$41.73

(1) _____

(2) _____

i.

Notes Payable	
$800.00	$4,200.00

(1) _____

(2) _____

j.

Notes Receivable	
$900.00	$213.50

(1) _____

(2) _____

6. Do Problem 6 on pages 435 to 436 of your textbook.

   a. Write your answers to Exercise 6a on the forms below and on the next page.

_____|_____

b. Answer Problem 6b below. Be sure the total debits equal the total credits.

Debits	=	**Credits**
_____		_____
_____		_____
_____		_____

Total _____ = Total _____

Do the total debits equal the total credits? _____

7. Do Problem 7 on page 436 of your textbook.

   a.–c. Write the answers to Problems 7a, 7b, and 7c on the forms below.

d. Answer Problem 7d in the spaces below.

Debits	=	Credits
_____		_____
_____		_____
_____		_____
_____		_____
_____		_____
Total _____	=	Total _____

Are the total debits and credits equal? _____

8. Do Problem 8 on pages 436 to 437 of your textbook.

   a.–c. Write your answers to Problems 8a, 8b, and 8c on the forms below.

d. Answer Problem 8d in the spaces below.

Debits	=	Credits
_____		_____
_____		_____
_____		_____
_____		_____
_____		_____

Total _____   =   Total _____

Are the total debits and credits equal? _____

CHAPTER 16

THE GENERAL JOURNAL AND LEDGER ACCOUNTS

TOPIC I ◆ THE GENERAL JOURNAL   Textbook pages 438 to 443

Check Your Reading

Use the spaces below to answer the questions on page 443 of your textbook.

1. _____
   _____

2. _____
   _____

3. _____

4. _____
   _____

5. a. _____
      _____
      _____

   b. _____

   c. _____

   d. _____
      _____
      _____

   e. _____

   f. _____

6. _____
   _____

7. _____

8. _____

9. _____

10. _____

Exercises for Topic 1

1. Do Exercise 1 on pages 443 to 444 of your textbook. Write your answers in the general journal below.

Helping Hint: Use the general journal entry illustrated on page 440 of your textbook as a model in completing this exercise.

GENERAL JOURNAL

Page 1

DATE		ACCOUNT TITLE AND EXPLANATION	POST. REF.	DEBIT	CREDIT

Check Your Work: Did you remember to list your debit account first? Do your debits equal your credits? If your answer to either of the above questions is no, correct your work.

2. Do Exercise 2 on page 444 of your textbook. Write your answers in the general journal below.

Helping Hint: Use the illustration on page 441 of your textbook as a model for an opening entry in a general journal.

GENERAL JOURNAL

Page 1

DATE		ACCOUNT TITLE AND EXPLANATION	POST. REF.	DEBIT	CREDIT

116

3. Do Exercise 3 on page 444 of your textbook. Answer below.

GENERAL JOURNAL   Page 1

DATE	ACCOUNT TITLE AND EXPLANATION	POST. REF.	DEBIT	CREDIT

4. Do Exercise 4 on pages 444 to 445 of your textbook. Answer below.

Helping Hint: Review page 442 of your textbook before beginning work.

GENERAL JOURNAL   Page 1

DATE	ACCOUNT TITLE AND EXPLANATION	POST. REF.	DEBIT	CREDIT

5. Do Exercise 5 on page 445 of your textbook. Write your answers on the form below.

GENERAL JOURNAL

DATE		ACCOUNT TITLE AND EXPLANATION	POST. REF.	DEBIT	CREDIT

Check Your Work: Do your debits equal your credits? If they do not, locate your error or errors.

Name _____

Date _____

TOPIC 2 ◆ LEDGER ACCOUNTS AND POSTING Textbook pages 445 to 450

Check Your Reading

Use the spaces below to answer the questions on page 450 of your textbook.

1. _____

2. _____

_____

_____

3. _____

4. a. _____

   b. _____

   c. _____

   _____

   d. _____

5. _____

Exercises for Topic 2

1. Do Exercise 1 on page 450 of your textbook. Write your answers on the ledger account forms below and on the next page of your Activity Guide.

Account No. _____

DATE	EXPLANATION	POST REF.	DEBIT	CREDIT	BALANCE DEBIT	BALANCE CREDIT

Account No. _____

DATE	EXPLANATION	POST REF.	DEBIT	CREDIT	BALANCE DEBIT	BALANCE CREDIT

Account No. _____

DATE	EXPLANATION	POST REF.	DEBIT	CREDIT	BALANCE DEBIT	BALANCE CREDIT

Account No. _____

DATE	EXPLANATION	POST REF.	DEBIT	CREDIT	BALANCE DEBIT	BALANCE CREDIT

			Account No.						

DATE	EXPLANATION	POST REF.	DEBIT	CREDIT	BALANCE	
					DEBIT	CREDIT

Account No.

DATE	EXPLANATION	POST REF.	DEBIT	CREDIT	BALANCE	
					DEBIT	CREDIT

2. Do Exercise 2 on pages 450 to 451 of your textbook. Write your answers on the ledger account forms below and on the next page of your Activity Guide.

Account No.

DATE	EXPLANATION	POST REF.	DEBIT	CREDIT	BALANCE	
					DEBIT	CREDIT

Account No.

DATE	EXPLANATION	POST REF.	DEBIT	CREDIT	BALANCE	
					DEBIT	CREDIT

Account No.

DATE	EXPLANATION	POST REF.	DEBIT	CREDIT	BALANCE	
					DEBIT	CREDIT

Account No.

DATE	EXPLANATION	POST REF.	DEBIT	CREDIT	BALANCE	
					DEBIT	CREDIT

Name _____

Date _____

Account No.

DATE	EXPLANATION	POST REF.	DEBIT	CREDIT	BALANCE	
					DEBIT	CREDIT

Account No.

DATE	EXPLANATION	POST REF.	DEBIT	CREDIT	BALANCE	
					DEBIT	CREDIT

Account No.

DATE	EXPLANATION	POST REF.	DEBIT	CREDIT	BALANCE	
					DEBIT	CREDIT

3. Do Exercise 3 on pages 451 to 452 of your textbook. Write your answers on the general journal below and on the ledger account forms on the following two pages of your Activity Guide.

GENERAL JOURNAL

Page 1

DATE		ACCOUNT TITLE AND EXPLANATION	POST. REF.	DEBIT	CREDIT

Name _____

Date _____

Account No. _____

DATE		EXPLANATION	POST REF.	DEBIT	CREDIT	BALANCE	
						DEBIT	CREDIT

Account No. _____

DATE		EXPLANATION	POST REF.	DEBIT	CREDIT	BALANCE	
						DEBIT	CREDIT

Account No. _____

DATE		EXPLANATION	POST REF.	DEBIT	CREDIT	BALANCE	
						DEBIT	CREDIT

Account No. _____

DATE		EXPLANATION	POST REF.	DEBIT	CREDIT	BALANCE	
						DEBIT	CREDIT

Account No. _____

DATE		EXPLANATION	POST REF.	DEBIT	CREDIT	BALANCE	
						DEBIT	CREDIT

Account No.

DATE		EXPLANATION	POST REF.	DEBIT	CREDIT	BALANCE	
						DEBIT	CREDIT

Account No.

DATE		EXPLANATION	POST REF.	DEBIT	CREDIT	BALANCE	
						DEBIT	CREDIT

Name _____

Date _____

END OF CHAPTER ACTIVITIES Textbook pages 453 to 455

Math Skillbuilder

Do the Math Skillbuilder on pages 453 to 454 of your textbook. Write your answers on the ledgers below.

1.

Accts. Pay. / Able Corp. _____ Account No. 223

DATE		EXPLANATION	POST REF.	DEBIT	CREDIT	BALANCE DEBIT	BALANCE CREDIT
Mar.¹⁹⁻	1	Opening entry	J1		950 00		
	2	Check 203	J1	450 00			
	3	Check 205	J1	500 00			
	5	Invoice 6221	J1		275 00		

2.

Accts. Pay. / Baker Corp. _____ Account No. 224

DATE		EXPLANATION	POST REF.	DEBIT	CREDIT	BALANCE DEBIT	BALANCE CREDIT
Mar.¹⁹⁻	1	Opening entry	J1		500 00		
	2	Check 204	J1	500 00			
	3	Invoice 7101	J1		320 00		

3.

Accts. Pay. / Delta Inc. _____ Account No. 225

DATE		EXPLANATION	POST REF.	DEBIT	CREDIT	BALANCE DEBIT	BALANCE CREDIT
Mar.¹⁹⁻	1	Opening entry	J1		100 00		
	2	Invoice 921	J1		1250 00		
	3	Credit memo	J1	400 00			
	5	Check 206	J1	850 00			

Vocabulary Skillbuilder

Do the Vocabulary Skillbuilder on page 454 of your textbook. Use the spaces below to write the term that best matches each statement.

1. _____

2. _____

3. _____

4. _____

5. _____

6. _____

7. _____

8. _____

9. _____

10. _____

11. _____

12. _____

Application Problems

I. Do Problem 1 on page 455 of your textbook. Write your answers on the form below.

GENERAL JOURNAL

Page 1

DATE	ACCOUNT TITLE AND EXPLANATION	POST. REF.	DEBIT	CREDIT

Note: Save your work for use in Problem 2.

2. Do Problem 2 on page 455 of your textbook. Write your answers on the ledger account forms below and on the next page of your Activity Guide.

Note: Save your work for use in Problem 4.

Account No.

DATE	EXPLANATION	POST REF.	DEBIT	CREDIT	BALANCE	
					DEBIT	CREDIT

Account No.

DATE	EXPLANATION	POST REF.	DEBIT	CREDIT	BALANCE	
					DEBIT	CREDIT

Account No.

DATE	EXPLANATION	POST REF.	DEBIT	CREDIT	BALANCE	
					DEBIT	CREDIT

Account No.

DATE	EXPLANATION	POST REF.	DEBIT	CREDIT	BALANCE	
					DEBIT	CREDIT

Date _____

Account No. _____

DATE	EXPLANATION	POST REF.	DEBIT	CREDIT	BALANCE	
					DEBIT	CREDIT

Account No. _____

DATE	EXPLANATION	POST REF.	DEBIT	CREDIT	BALANCE	
					DEBIT	CREDIT

Account No. _____

DATE	EXPLANATION	POST REF.	DEBIT	CREDIT	BALANCE	
					DEBIT	CREDIT

Account No. _____

DATE	EXPLANATION	POST REF.	DEBIT	CREDIT	BALANCE	
					DEBIT	CREDIT

3. Do Problem 3 on page 455 of your textbook. Write your answers on the form below.

GENERAL JOURNAL

Page 2

DATE	ACCOUNT TITLE AND EXPLANATION	POST. REF.	DEBIT	CREDIT

Note: Save your work for use in Problem 4.

4. Do Problem 4 on page 455 of your textbook. Write your answers on the ledger account forms on pages 122 and 123 of your Activity Guide, which you prepared in Problem 2.

CHAPTER 17   Date _____

SPECIAL JOURNALS: PURCHASES AND CASH PAYMENTS

TOPIC 1 ◆ JOURNALIZING AND POSTING PURCHASES   Textbook pages 456 to 463

Check Your Reading

Use the spaces below to answer the questions on page 463 of your textbook.

1. _____
   _____
2. _____
3. _____
4. _____
5. _____
6. _____
7. _____

Exercises for Topic 1

1. Do Exercise 1 on page 464 of your textbook. Write your answers on the form below.

Helping Hint: Review page 461 of your textbook before beginning this exercise.

PURCHASES JOURNAL   Page   1

DATE	INVOICE NO.	ACCOUNT CREDITED	POST. REF.	PURCHASES DEBIT

2. Do Exercise 2 on page 464 of your textbook. Write the answers on the forms below and on the next page of your Activity Guide and on the purchases journal on page 125, which you prepared in Exercise 1.

Account No. _____

DATE	EXPLANATION	POST REF.	DEBIT	CREDIT	BALANCE DEBIT	BALANCE CREDIT

Account No. _____

DATE	EXPLANATION	POST REF.	DEBIT	CREDIT	BALANCE DEBIT	BALANCE CREDIT

Account No. _____

DATE	EXPLANATION	POST REF.	DEBIT	CREDIT	BALANCE DEBIT	BALANCE CREDIT

Account No. _____

DATE	EXPLANATION	POST REF.	DEBIT	CREDIT	BALANCE DEBIT	BALANCE CREDIT

Account No. _____

DATE	EXPLANATION	POST REF.	DEBIT	CREDIT	BALANCE DEBIT	BALANCE CREDIT

Account No. _____

DATE	EXPLANATION	POST REF.	DEBIT	CREDIT	BALANCE DEBIT	BALANCE CREDIT

© by Glencoe.

Name _____

Date _____

Account No. _____

DATE	EXPLANATION	POST REF.	DEBIT	CREDIT	BALANCE	
					DEBIT	CREDIT

Account No. _____

DATE	EXPLANATION	POST REF.	DEBIT	CREDIT	BALANCE	
					DEBIT	CREDIT

3. Do Exercise 3 on pages 464 to 465 of your textbook. Write your answers on the forms below.

PURCHASES JOURNAL   Page 1

DATE	INVOICE NO.	ACCOUNT CREDITED	POST. REF.	PURCHASES DEBIT

GENERAL JOURNAL   Page 1

DATE	ACCOUNT TITLE AND EXPLANATION	POST. REF.	DEBIT	CREDIT

4. Do Exercise 4 on page 465 of your textbook. Write your answers on the forms on page 128 of your Activity Guide and on the purchases journal and general journal above.

DATE		EXPLANATION	POST REF.	DEBIT	CREDIT	BALANCE	
						DEBIT	CREDIT

Account No.

DATE		EXPLANATION	POST REF.	DEBIT	CREDIT	BALANCE	
						DEBIT	CREDIT

Account No.

DATE		EXPLANATION	POST REF.	DEBIT	CREDIT	BALANCE	
						DEBIT	CREDIT

5. Do Exercise 5 on page 465 of your textbook. Answer below.

Account No.

DATE		EXPLANATION	POST REF.	DEBIT	CREDIT	BALANCE	
						DEBIT	CREDIT

Account No.

DATE		EXPLANATION	POST REF.	DEBIT	CREDIT	BALANCE	
						DEBIT	CREDIT

Account No.

DATE		EXPLANATION	POST REF.	DEBIT	CREDIT	BALANCE	
						DEBIT	CREDIT

Account No.

DATE		EXPLANATION	POST REF.	DEBIT	CREDIT	BALANCE	
						DEBIT	CREDIT

Name _____

Date _____

TOPIC 2 ◆ JOURNALIZING AND POSTING CASH PAYMENTS
Textbook pages 465 to 470

Check Your Reading

Use the spaces below to answer the questions on page 470 of your textbook.

1. _____   _____
2. _____   _____
3. _____   _____
4. _____   _____
5. _____   _____
6. _____   _____

Exercises for Topic 2

1. Do Exercise 1 on pages 470 to 471 of your textbook. Write your answers below.

CASH PAYMENTS JOURNAL   Page 1

DATE	ACCOUNT DEBITED	CHECK NO.	POST. REF.	CASH CREDIT

Note: Remember to save your work for use in Exercise 2.

2. Do Exercise 2 on pages 471 to 472 of your textbook. Use the forms below and on the next page.

Account No. _____

DATE	EXPLANATION	POST REF.	DEBIT	CREDIT	BALANCE DEBIT	BALANCE CREDIT

Account No. _____

DATE	EXPLANATION	POST REF.	DEBIT	CREDIT	BALANCE DEBIT	BALANCE CREDIT

Account No. _____

DATE	EXPLANATION	POST REF.	DEBIT	CREDIT	BALANCE DEBIT	BALANCE CREDIT

Account No. _____

DATE	EXPLANATION	POST REF.	DEBIT	CREDIT	BALANCE DEBIT	BALANCE CREDIT

Account No. _____

DATE	EXPLANATION	POST REF.	DEBIT	CREDIT	BALANCE DEBIT	BALANCE CREDIT

Account No. _____

DATE	EXPLANATION	POST REF.	DEBIT	CREDIT	BALANCE DEBIT	BALANCE CREDIT

Name _____

Date _____

Account No. _____

DATE	EXPLANATION	POST REF.	DEBIT	CREDIT	BALANCE	
					DEBIT	CREDIT

Account No. _____

DATE	EXPLANATION	POST REF.	DEBIT	CREDIT	BALANCE	
					DEBIT	CREDIT

Account No. _____

DATE	EXPLANATION	POST REF.	DEBIT	CREDIT	BALANCE	
					DEBIT	CREDIT

Account No. _____

DATE	EXPLANATION	POST REF.	DEBIT	CREDIT	BALANCE	
					DEBIT	CREDIT

Account No. _____

DATE	EXPLANATION	POST REF.	DEBIT	CREDIT	BALANCE	
					DEBIT	CREDIT

3. Do Exercise 3 on page 472 of your textbook. Write your answers on the forms below and on the next page.

Account No. _____

DATE	EXPLANATION	POST REF.	DEBIT	CREDIT	BALANCE	
					DEBIT	CREDIT

DATE		EXPLANATION	POST REF.	DEBIT	CREDIT	BALANCE	
						DEBIT	CREDIT

DATE		EXPLANATION	POST REF.	DEBIT	CREDIT	BALANCE	
						DEBIT	CREDIT

DATE		EXPLANATION	POST REF.	DEBIT	CREDIT	BALANCE	
						DEBIT	CREDIT

CASH PAYMENTS JOURNAL   Page 1

DATE		ACCOUNT DEBITED	CHECK NO.	POST. REF.	CASH CREDIT

Name _____

Date _____

END OF CHAPTER ACTIVITIES   Textbook pages 473 to 475

Vocabulary Skillbuilder

Do the Vocabulary Skillbuilder on pages 473 to 474 of your textbook. Use the spaces below to write the term that best matches each statement.

1. _____
2. _____
3. _____
4. _____
5. _____
6. _____
7. _____
8. _____
9. _____
10. _____
11. _____
12. _____
13. _____
14. _____
15. _____
16. _____
17. _____
18. _____
19. _____
20. _____

Application Problems

1. Do Problem 1 on page 474 of your textbook. Write your answers on the forms below.

PURCHASES JOURNAL   Page 1

DATE	INVOICE NO.	ACCOUNT CREDITED	POST. REF.	PURCHASES DEBIT

GENERAL JOURNAL   Page 1

DATE	ACCOUNT TITLE AND EXPLANATION	POST. REF.	DEBIT	CREDIT

Date _____

2. Do Problem 2 on page 474 of your textbook. Write your answers on the forms below and on the next page of your Activity Guide.

Account No. _____

DATE	EXPLANATION	POST REF.	DEBIT	CREDIT	BALANCE DEBIT	CREDIT

Account No. _____

DATE	EXPLANATION	POST REF.	DEBIT	CREDIT	BALANCE DEBIT	CREDIT

Account No. _____

DATE	EXPLANATION	POST REF.	DEBIT	CREDIT	BALANCE DEBIT	CREDIT

Account No. _____

DATE	EXPLANATION	POST REF.	DEBIT	CREDIT	BALANCE DEBIT	CREDIT

DATE	EXPLANATION	POST REF.	DEBIT	CREDIT	BALANCE	
					DEBIT	CREDIT

3. Do Problem 3 on pages 474 to 475 of your textbook. Write your answers on the forms below and on the next three pages.

DATE	EXPLANATION	POST REF.	DEBIT	CREDIT	BALANCE	
					DEBIT	CREDIT

DATE	EXPLANATION	POST REF.	DEBIT	CREDIT	BALANCE	
					DEBIT	CREDIT

Date _____

Account No. _____

DATE	EXPLANATION	POST REF.	DEBIT	CREDIT	BALANCE	
					DEBIT	CREDIT

Account No. _____

DATE	EXPLANATION	POST REF.	DEBIT	CREDIT	BALANCE	
					DEBIT	CREDIT

Account No. _____

DATE	EXPLANATION	POST REF.	DEBIT	CREDIT	BALANCE	
					DEBIT	CREDIT

Account No. _____

DATE	EXPLANATION	POST REF.	DEBIT	CREDIT	BALANCE	
					DEBIT	CREDIT

© by Glencoe.

Account No.

DATE		EXPLANATION	POST REF.	DEBIT	CREDIT	BALANCE	
						DEBIT	CREDIT

Account No.

DATE		EXPLANATION	POST REF.	DEBIT	CREDIT	BALANCE	
						DEBIT	CREDIT

Account No.

DATE		EXPLANATION	POST REF.	DEBIT	CREDIT	BALANCE	
						DEBIT	CREDIT

Account No.

DATE		EXPLANATION	POST REF.	DEBIT	CREDIT	BALANCE	
						DEBIT	CREDIT

Date _____

CASH PAYMENTS JOURNAL

Page 1

DATE	ACCOUNT DEBITED	CHECK NO.	POST. REF.	CASH CREDIT

4. Do Problem 4 on page 475 of your textbook. Write your answers on the forms below and on the next page.

Account No. _____

DATE		EXPLANATION	POST REF.	DEBIT	CREDIT	BALANCE	
						DEBIT	CREDIT

Account No. _____

DATE		EXPLANATION	POST REF.	DEBIT	CREDIT	BALANCE	
						DEBIT	CREDIT

Account No. _____

DATE		EXPLANATION	POST REF.	DEBIT	CREDIT	BALANCE	
						DEBIT	CREDIT

Account No. _____

DATE		EXPLANATION	POST REF.	DEBIT	CREDIT	BALANCE	
						DEBIT	CREDIT

Account No. _____

DATE		EXPLANATION	POST REF.	DEBIT	CREDIT	BALANCE	
						DEBIT	CREDIT

Account No. _____

DATE		EXPLANATION	POST REF.	DEBIT	CREDIT	BALANCE	
						DEBIT	CREDIT

Account No. _____

DATE		EXPLANATION	POST REF.	DEBIT	CREDIT	BALANCE	
						DEBIT	CREDIT

5. Do Problem 5 on page 475 of your textbook. Answer below.

PURCHASES JOURNAL

DATE		INVOICE NO.	ACCOUNT CREDITED	POST. REF.	PURCHASES DEBIT

CASH PAYMENTS JOURNAL

DATE		ACCOUNT DEBITED	CHECK NO.	POST. REF.	CASH CREDIT

CHAPTER 18

SPECIAL JOURNALS: SALES AND CASH RECEIPTS

TOPIC 1 ◆ JOURNALIZING AND POSTING SALES   Textbook pages 476 to 482

Check Your Reading

Use the spaces below to answer the questions on page 482 of your textbook.

1. _____   5. _____
2. _____   6. _____
3. _____   7. _____
4. _____   8. _____

Exercises for Topic 1

1. Do Exercise 1 on pages 482 to 483 of your textbook. Write your answers on the form below.

Helping Hint: Use the illustration on page 479 of your textbook as a model in doing this exercise.

SALES JOURNAL   Page 1

DATE	SALES SLIP NO.	ACCOUNT DEBITED	POST. REF.	SALES CREDIT

Note: Remember to save your work for use in Exercise 2.

2. Do Exercise 2 on page 483 of your textbook. Write your answers on the forms below and on the following page.

Account No. ____

DATE		EXPLANATION	POST REF.	DEBIT	CREDIT	BALANCE	
						DEBIT	CREDIT

Account No. ____

DATE		EXPLANATION	POST REF.	DEBIT	CREDIT	BALANCE	
						DEBIT	CREDIT

Account No. ____

DATE		EXPLANATION	POST REF.	DEBIT	CREDIT	BALANCE	
						DEBIT	CREDIT

Account No. ____

DATE		EXPLANATION	POST REF.	DEBIT	CREDIT	BALANCE	
						DEBIT	CREDIT

Name _____

Date _____

Account No. _____

DATE	EXPLANATION	POST REF.	DEBIT	CREDIT	BALANCE	
					DEBIT	CREDIT

Account No. _____

DATE	EXPLANATION	POST REF.	DEBIT	CREDIT	BALANCE	
					DEBIT	CREDIT

3. Do Exercise 3 on page 483 of your textbook. Write your answers on the forms below and on the next page.

Account No. _____

DATE	EXPLANATION	POST REF.	DEBIT	CREDIT	BALANCE	
					DEBIT	CREDIT

Account No. _____

DATE	EXPLANATION	POST REF.	DEBIT	CREDIT	BALANCE	
					DEBIT	CREDIT

DATE		EXPLANATION	POST REF.	DEBIT	CREDIT	BALANCE	
						DEBIT	CREDIT

Account No.

DATE		EXPLANATION	POST REF.	DEBIT	CREDIT	BALANCE	
						DEBIT	CREDIT

4. Do Exercise 4 on pages 483 to 484 of your textbook. Write your answers on the forms below and on the next two pages.

Account No.

DATE		EXPLANATION	POST REF.	DEBIT	CREDIT	BALANCE	
						DEBIT	CREDIT

Account No.

DATE		EXPLANATION	POST REF.	DEBIT	CREDIT	BALANCE	
						DEBIT	CREDIT

Name _____

Date _____

Account No. _____

DATE		EXPLANATION	POST REF.	DEBIT	CREDIT	BALANCE	
						DEBIT	CREDIT

SALES JOURNAL

Page 1

DATE		SALES SLIP NO.	ACCOUNT DEBITED	POST. REF.	SALES CREDIT

DATE	ACCOUNT TITLE AND EXPLANATION	POST. REF.	DEBIT	CREDIT

EXTRA FORMS

Account No.

DATE	EXPLANATION	POST REF.	DEBIT	CREDIT	BALANCE DEBIT	CREDIT

Account No.

DATE	EXPLANATION	POST REF.	DEBIT	CREDIT	BALANCE DEBIT	CREDIT

Name _____

Date _____

TOPIC 2 ◆ JOURNALIZING AND POSTING CASH RECEIPTS
Textbook pages 484 to 487

Check Your Reading

Use the spaces below to answer the questions on page 487 of your textbook.

1. _____   **4.** _____

2. _____   **5.** _____

3. _____   **6.** _____

Exercises for Topic 2

1. Do Exercise 1 on pages 487 to 488 of your textbook. Answer below.

Helping Hint: Use the illustration on page 486 of your textbook as a model.

CASH RECEIPTS JOURNAL   **Page** *1*

DATE		ACCOUNT CREDITED	POST. REF.	CASH DEBIT

Note: Save your work for use in Exercise 2.

2. Do Exercise 2 on page 488 of your textbook. Write your answers on the forms below and on the following page and in the cash receipts journal on the preceding page, which you prepared for Exercise 1.

Helping Hint: Use the illustration on page 486 of your textbook as a model. Use the date September 30 for the total of the cash receipts journal.

Account No. _____

DATE	EXPLANATION	POST REF.	DEBIT	CREDIT	BALANCE DEBIT	CREDIT

Account No. _____

DATE	EXPLANATION	POST REF.	DEBIT	CREDIT	BALANCE DEBIT	CREDIT

Account No. _____

DATE	EXPLANATION	POST REF.	DEBIT	CREDIT	BALANCE DEBIT	CREDIT

Account No. _____

DATE	EXPLANATION	POST REF.	DEBIT	CREDIT	BALANCE DEBIT	CREDIT

Name _____

Date _____

Account No. _____

DATE		EXPLANATION	POST REF.	DEBIT	CREDIT	BALANCE	
						DEBIT	CREDIT

Account No. _____

DATE		EXPLANATION	POST REF.	DEBIT	CREDIT	BALANCE	
						DEBIT	CREDIT

Account No. _____

DATE		EXPLANATION	POST REF.	DEBIT	CREDIT	BALANCE	
						DEBIT	CREDIT

3. Do Exercise 3 on pages 488 and 489 of your textbook. Write your answers on the forms below and on the next two pages.

Account No. ___

DATE	EXPLANATION	POST REF.	DEBIT	CREDIT	BALANCE	
					DEBIT	CREDIT

Account No. ___

DATE	EXPLANATION	POST REF.	DEBIT	CREDIT	BALANCE	
					DEBIT	CREDIT

Account No. ___

DATE	EXPLANATION	POST REF.	DEBIT	CREDIT	BALANCE	
					DEBIT	CREDIT

Account No. ___

DATE	EXPLANATION	POST REF.	DEBIT	CREDIT	BALANCE	
					DEBIT	CREDIT

Name _____

Date _____

Account No. _____

DATE	EXPLANATION	POST REF.	DEBIT	CREDIT	BALANCE	
					DEBIT	CREDIT

Account No. _____

DATE	EXPLANATION	POST REF.	DEBIT	CREDIT	BALANCE	
					DEBIT	CREDIT

Account No. _____

DATE	EXPLANATION	POST REF.	DEBIT	CREDIT	BALANCE	
					DEBIT	CREDIT

DATE		ACCOUNT CREDITED	POST. REF.	CASH DEBIT

Name _____

Date _____

TOPIC 3 ◆ PROVING CASH Textbook pages 489 to 490

Check Your Reading

Use the spaces below to answer the questions on page 490 of your textbook.

1. _____

   _____

   _____

   _____

   _____

2. _____

   _____

   _____

3. _____

Exercises for Topic 3

1. Do Exercise 1 on pages 491 and 492 of your textbook. Write your answers on the forms below and on the next four pages.

Account No. _____

DATE		EXPLANATION	POST REF.	DEBIT	CREDIT	BALANCE	
						DEBIT	CREDIT

Account No. _____

DATE		EXPLANATION	POST REF.	DEBIT	CREDIT	BALANCE	
						DEBIT	CREDIT

Account No.

DATE		EXPLANATION	POST REF.	DEBIT	CREDIT	BALANCE	
						DEBIT	CREDIT

Account No.

DATE		EXPLANATION	POST REF.	DEBIT	CREDIT	BALANCE	
						DEBIT	CREDIT

Account No.

DATE		EXPLANATION	POST REF.	DEBIT	CREDIT	BALANCE	
						DEBIT	CREDIT

Name _____

Date _____

Account No.

DATE	EXPLANATION	POST REF.	DEBIT	CREDIT	BALANCE DEBIT	CREDIT

Account No.

DATE	EXPLANATION	POST REF.	DEBIT	CREDIT	BALANCE DEBIT	CREDIT

Account No.

DATE	EXPLANATION	POST REF.	DEBIT	CREDIT	BALANCE DEBIT	CREDIT

Account No.

DATE	EXPLANATION	POST REF.	DEBIT	CREDIT	BALANCE DEBIT	CREDIT

DATE		EXPLANATION	POST REF.	DEBIT	CREDIT	BALANCE	
						DEBIT	CREDIT

DATE		EXPLANATION	POST REF.	DEBIT	CREDIT	BALANCE	
						DEBIT	CREDIT

CASH RECEIPTS JOURNAL   Page 1

DATE		ACCOUNT CREDITED	POST. REF.	CASH DEBIT

Name _____

Date _____

CASH PAYMENTS JOURNAL   Page 1

DATE		ACCOUNT DEBITED	CHECK NO.	POST. REF.	CASH CREDIT

Use the space below to prepare a cash proof.

_____

_____

_____

_____

_____

_____

Check Your Work: Did your ending cash balance equal the checkbook balance of $9,707.46? If not, locate your error or errors.

Learning Through Practice

Below is a form with four money columns. Amounts to be entered on the form are to the left of the form. The classification for each amount tells you which column of the form to use. Enter each amount in the proper column. The first amount has been done as an example. After you have entered all the amounts, total each column of the form. Then add the totals of the four columns.

Classification	Amount	PURCHASES JOURNAL	CASH PAYMENTS JOURNAL	SALES JOURNAL	CASH RECEIPTS JOURNAL
Purchase	6,524.50	6524 50			
Sale	4,229.65				
Cash payment	912.43				
Cash payment	3,654.90				
Purchase	4,576.22				
Sale	1,650.00				
Cash payment	5,459.50				
Cash receipt	11,040.50				
Sale	10,950.75				
Purchase	2,354.85				
Cash payment	6,040.40				
Sale	12,346.72				
Cash receipt	7,225.46				
Cash payment	1,243.55				
Cash receipt	1,542.09				
Purchase	6,464.25				
Sale	8,050.50				
Cash receipt	9,250.42				
Totals					

Total of the four columns: _____

Check Your Work: Does the total of the four columns equal $103,516.69? If not, locate your error or errors.

Name _____

Date _____

TOPIC 4 ◆ MULTICOLUMN CASH JOURNALS Textbook pages 492 to 496

Check Your Reading

Use the spaces below to answer the questions on pages 496 to 497 of your textbook.

1. a. _____

_____

_____

_____

b. _____

_____

_____

_____

c. _____

_____

_____

_____

2. a. _____

_____

_____

_____

b. _____

_____

_____

_____

c. _____

_____

_____

_____

Exercises for Topic 4

I. Do Exercise 1 on pages 497 to 498 of your textbook. Write your answers on the forms below and on the following four pages.

Helping Hint: Review the illustrations on pages 486 to 493 of your textbook before beginning this exercise.

Account No. _____

DATE	EXPLANATION	POST REF.	DEBIT	CREDIT	BALANCE DEBIT	BALANCE CREDIT

Account No. _____

DATE	EXPLANATION	POST REF.	DEBIT	CREDIT	BALANCE DEBIT	BALANCE CREDIT

Account No. _____

DATE	EXPLANATION	POST REF.	DEBIT	CREDIT	BALANCE DEBIT	BALANCE CREDIT

Account No. _____

DATE	EXPLANATION	POST REF.	DEBIT	CREDIT	BALANCE DEBIT	BALANCE CREDIT

Name _____

Date _____

Account No.

DATE	EXPLANATION	POST REF.	DEBIT	CREDIT	BALANCE	
					DEBIT	CREDIT

Account No.

DATE	EXPLANATION	POST REF.	DEBIT	CREDIT	BALANCE	
					DEBIT	CREDIT

Account No.

DATE	EXPLANATION	POST REF.	DEBIT	CREDIT	BALANCE	
					DEBIT	CREDIT

Account No.

DATE	EXPLANATION	POST REF.	DEBIT	CREDIT	BALANCE	
					DEBIT	CREDIT

DATE		EXPLANATION	POST REF.	DEBIT	CREDIT	BALANCE	
						DEBIT	CREDIT

DATE		EXPLANATION	POST REF.	DEBIT	CREDIT	BALANCE	
						DEBIT	CREDIT

DATE		EXPLANATION	POST REF.	DEBIT	CREDIT	BALANCE	
						DEBIT	CREDIT

DATE		EXPLANATION	POST REF.	DEBIT	CREDIT	BALANCE	
						DEBIT	CREDIT

Name _____

Date _____

CASH RECEIPTS JOURNAL

DATE	ACCOUNT CREDITED	POST. REF.	GENERAL LEDGER CREDIT	SALES CREDIT	REPAIR REVENUE CREDIT	NET CASH DEBIT

Use the space below to prove cash.

_____

_____

_____

_____

_____

_____

CASH PAYMENTS JOURNAL

DATE	ACCOUNT DEBITED	CHECK NO.	POST. REF.	GENERAL LEDGER DEBIT	PURCHASES DEBIT	STORE EXPENSE DEBIT	NET CASH CREDIT

Name _____

Date _____

END OF CHAPTER ACTIVITIES Textbook pages 499 to 501

Vocabulary Skillbuilder

Do the Vocabulary Skillbuilder on page 499 of your textbook. Use the spaces below to write the term that best matches each statement.

1. _____
2. _____
3. _____
4. _____
5. _____
6. _____
7. _____
8. _____
9. _____
10. _____
11. _____
12. _____
13. _____
14. _____
15. _____
16. _____
17. _____

Application Problems

I. Do Problem 1 on page 500 of your textbook. Write your answers on the forms below and on the next page.

Account No. _____

DATE	EXPLANATION	POST REF.	DEBIT	CREDIT	BALANCE DEBIT	BALANCE CREDIT

Account No. _____

DATE	EXPLANATION	POST REF.	DEBIT	CREDIT	BALANCE DEBIT	BALANCE CREDIT

Account No. _____

DATE	EXPLANATION	POST REF.	DEBIT	CREDIT	BALANCE DEBIT	BALANCE CREDIT

Account No. _____

DATE	EXPLANATION	POST REF.	DEBIT	CREDIT	BALANCE DEBIT	BALANCE CREDIT

SALES JOURNAL   Page 1

DATE	SALES SLIP NO.	ACCOUNT DEBITED	POST. REF.	SALES CREDIT

GENERAL JOURNAL   Page 1

DATE	ACCOUNT TITLE AND EXPLANATION	POST. REF.	DEBIT	CREDIT

2. Do Problem 2 on pages 500 to 501 of your textbook. Write your answers for Problem 2 on the forms below and on the following five pages.

Account No.

DATE		EXPLANATION	POST REF.	DEBIT	CREDIT	BALANCE	
						DEBIT	CREDIT

Account No.

DATE		EXPLANATION	POST REF.	DEBIT	CREDIT	BALANCE	
						DEBIT	CREDIT

Account No.

DATE		EXPLANATION	POST REF.	DEBIT	CREDIT	BALANCE	
						DEBIT	CREDIT

Account No.

DATE		EXPLANATION	POST REF.	DEBIT	CREDIT	BALANCE	
						DEBIT	CREDIT

Account No. _____

DATE		EXPLANATION	POST REF.	DEBIT	CREDIT	BALANCE	
						DEBIT	CREDIT

Account No. _____

DATE		EXPLANATION	POST REF.	DEBIT	CREDIT	BALANCE	
						DEBIT	CREDIT

Account No. _____

DATE		EXPLANATION	POST REF.	DEBIT	CREDIT	BALANCE	
						DEBIT	CREDIT

Account No. _____

DATE		EXPLANATION	POST REF.	DEBIT	CREDIT	BALANCE	
						DEBIT	CREDIT

DATE	EXPLANATION	POST REF.	DEBIT	CREDIT	BALANCE	
					DEBIT	CREDIT

DATE	EXPLANATION	POST REF.	DEBIT	CREDIT	BALANCE	
					DEBIT	CREDIT

DATE	EXPLANATION	POST REF.	DEBIT	CREDIT	BALANCE	
					DEBIT	CREDIT

DATE	EXPLANATION	POST REF.	DEBIT	CREDIT	BALANCE	
					DEBIT	CREDIT

Account No.

DATE	EXPLANATION	POST REF.	DEBIT	CREDIT	BALANCE	
					DEBIT	CREDIT

Account No.

DATE	EXPLANATION	POST REF.	DEBIT	CREDIT	BALANCE	
					DEBIT	CREDIT

Account No.

DATE	EXPLANATION	POST REF.	DEBIT	CREDIT	BALANCE	
					DEBIT	CREDIT

Account No.

DATE	EXPLANATION	POST REF.	DEBIT	CREDIT	BALANCE	
					DEBIT	CREDIT

Account No.

DATE	EXPLANATION	POST REF.	DEBIT	CREDIT	BALANCE	
					DEBIT	CREDIT

PURCHASES JOURNAL

Page 1

DATE	INVOICE NO.	ACCOUNT CREDITED	POST. REF.	PURCHASES DEBIT

CASH PAYMENTS JOURNAL

Page 1

DATE	ACCOUNT DEBITED	CHECK NO.	POST. REF.	CASH CREDIT

Date _____

SALES JOURNAL
Page 1

DATE	SALES SLIP NO.	ACCOUNT DEBITED	POST. REF.	SALES CREDIT

CASH RECEIPTS JOURNAL
Page 1

DATE	ACCOUNT CREDITED	POST. REF.	CASH DEBIT

Use the space below to prove cash.

_____

_____

_____

_____

_____

Learning Through Practice

As the accounting clerk for the Varsity Sports Center, you must prepare the departmental sales report for May. The report shows the sales made by each department for May of this year and for May of last year. The report also shows the amount of increase or decrease in sales from last year. The departmental sales report used by Varsity Sports Center is given below.

Varsity Sports Center
Departmental Sales Report
Month of _____ 19 __

Department	Sales				Amount of			
	This Year		Last Year		Increase		Decrease	
Athletics	2,753	82	2,673	54	80	28		
Camping								
Hobby Corner								
Hunting								
Toys								
Water Sports								
TOTALS								
Net Increase or Decrease	/////////							

You must enter the following information on the departmental sales report:

Athletics: This year, $2,753.82; last year, $2,673.54.
Camping: This year, $3,834.67; last year, $3,878.24.
Hobby Corner: This year, $1,590.29; last year, $1,599.80.
Hunting: This year, $3,968.47; last year, $3,893.24.
Toys: This year, $1,676.30; last year, $1,690.83.
Water Sports: This year, $1,427.65; last year, $1,386.47.

After you enter all the information, total the four columns. Then find the net increase or decrease of sales for all departments for the month of May.

Helping Hint: The figures for the athletics department for the month of May have been entered as an example. Note the sales for May of this year are more than the sales for May of last year. That means there has been an increase in sales. The difference, $80.28 ($2,753.82 − $2,673.54 = $80.28), is entered in the Increase column. If the monthly sales for this year had been less than those of last year, the difference would have been entered in the Decrease column.

CHAPTER 19

THE TRIAL BALANCE AND FINANCIAL STATEMENTS

TOPIC 1 ♦ THE TRIAL BALANCE   Textbook pages 502 to 509

Check Your Reading

Use the spaces below to answer the questions on page 509 of your textbook.

1. _____   4. _____

2. _____   5. _____

3. _____   6. _____

Exercises for Topic 1

1. Do Exercise 1 on pages 509 to 510 of your textbook. Write your answers on the form below.

Helping Hint: Use the illustration on page 506 of your textbook as a model in preparing your trial balance.

ACCOUNT TITLE	ACCT. NO.	DEBIT	CREDIT

2. Do Exercise 2 on page 510 of your textbook. Write your answers on the form below.

ACCOUNT TITLE	ACCT. NO.	DEBIT	CREDIT

Name _____

Date _____

TOPIC 2 ◆ FINANCIAL STATEMENTS FOR A SERVICE BUSINESS
Textbook pages 511 to 516

Check Your Reading

Use the spaces below to answer the questions on page 516 of your textbook.

1. a. _____ f. _____

   b. _____ g. _____

   c. _____ h. _____

   d. _____ i. _____

   e. _____ j. _____

2.

Account	Type of Balance
a. Notes Payable	_____
b. Miscellaneous Expenses	_____
c. Delivery Equipment	_____
d. Salaries Expense	_____
e. Rosa Dunn, Capital	_____
f. Office Furniture	_____
g. Delivery Revenue	_____
h. Supplies Expense	_____
i. Cash	_____
j. Rent Expense	_____

3. _____
   _____

4. _____

5. _____
   _____
   _____
   _____

6. _____
   _____

Exercises for Topic 2

I. Do Exercise 1 on page 517 of your textbook.

    a. Write your answers for Exercise 1a below.

Account	Classification	Type of Balance

    b. Write your answers for Exercise 1b below.

Account	Classification	Type of Balance

2. Do Exercise 2 on page 517 of your textbook. Answer below.

Account	Classification	Type of Balance

3. Do Exercise 3 on page 518 of your textbook. Answer below.

   a. Helping Hint: Use the illustration on page 513 of your textbook as a model.

_____

_____

   b. Helping Hint: Use the illustration of the balance sheet on page 515 of your textbook to help you do this balance sheet. The account receivable has been recorded for you as an example. Record the account payable in a similar way.

_____

_____

Accounts Receivable:				
Jane Redmond	4 0 0 00			

Check Your Work: Did you remember to add Net Income to the Capital account? Does the total of the left side equal the total of the right side? If your answer to either of these questions is no, locate your error or errors.

4. Do Exercise 4 on page 518 of your textbook. Answer below.

a.

b.

Name _____

Date _____

5. Do Exercise 5 on page 518 of your textbook. Answer below.

a.

_____
_____

b.

_____
_____

Learning Through Practice

Groups of items are listed below. Do one group at a time, and find the classification of each item in the group. After each group, write the name of the item that does not belong in that group. Then explain why the item does not belong. Number 1 is completed as an example.

1. Cash

    Delivery Equipment

    Notes Payable

1. Does not belong: <u>Notes Payable. Cash and</u> <u>equipment are asset accounts; notes payable</u> <u>is a liability.</u>

2. Rent Expense

    Cash

    Delivery Equipment

2. Does not belong: _____

3. Rental Revenue

    Cash

    Farm Revenue

3. Does not belong: _____

4. Miscellaneous Expenses

    Advertising Expense

    Fees Revenue

    Rent Expense

4. Does not belong: _____

5. Rent Revenue

    Insurance Expense

    Delivery Revenue

5. Does not belong: _____

6. Accts. Rec./Dunn Wholesale Co.

    Accts. Pay./Quimby Hobby Shop

    Accts. Pay./Betty Bixby

6. Does not belong: _____

7. Cash

    Office Furniture

    Notes Payable

7. Does not belong: _____

8. Rent Revenue

    Salaries Expense

    Miscellaneous Expenses

8. Does not belong: _____

Name _____

Date _____

TOPIC 3 ◆ FINANCIAL STATEMENTS FOR A MERCHANDISING BUSINESS Textbook pages 520 to 526

Check Your Reading

Use the spaces below to answer the questions on page 526 of your textbook.

1. _____
   _____
   _____
   _____

2. _____
   _____
   _____
   _____
   _____

3. _____
   _____
   _____
   _____

4. _____
   _____
   _____
   _____
   _____
   _____

5. _____
   _____
   _____
   _____

6. _____

7. _____

Exercise for Topic 3

1. Do Exercise 1 on page 526 of your textbook. Write your answers on the forms below.

    a. Helping Hint: Use the illustration on page 525 of your textbook as a model in working this exercise.

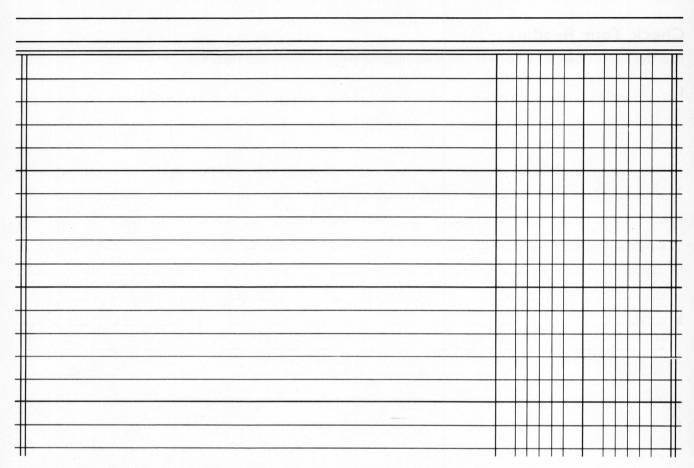

    b. Helping Hint: Use the illustration on page 525 of your textbook as a model. You will need the income statement above and the trial balance on textbook page 527.

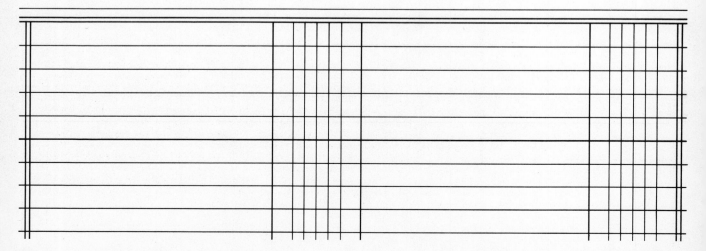

Name _____

Date _____

2. Do Exercise 2 on page 526 of your textbook. Write your answers on the forms below.

a.

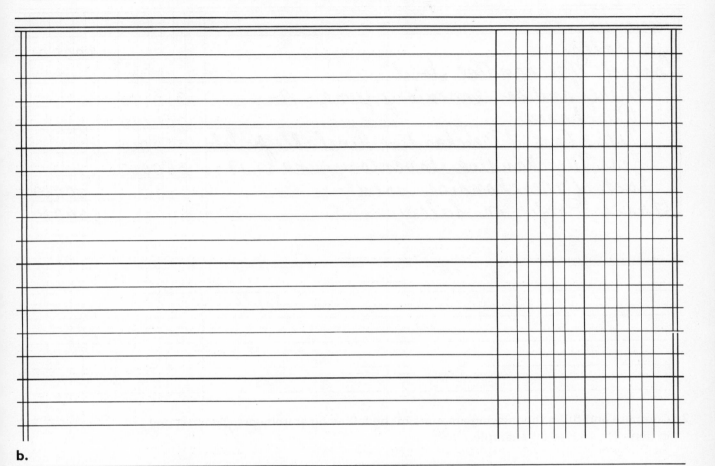

b.

Learning Through Practice

1. Below is part of an income statement. See if you can locate any errors. List any errors you find on the lines below the statement.

Janette's Gift Shop
June 30, 19—
Income Statement

Revenue:			
Sales			8000 00
Cost of Merchandise Sold:			
Merchandise Inventory, June 1, 19—		3100 00	
Purchases		2000 00	
Total Cost of Merchandise Available for Sale		5100 00	
Less Merchandise Inventory, June 30, 19—		3500 00	
Cost of Merchandise Sold			1600 00
Gross Profit on Sales			9600 00

_____

_____

_____

_____

_____

_____

2. Compute and fill in the missing amounts in the following statements. The first one is done for you as an example.

	Beginning Inventory	+	Purchases	=	Merchandise Available for Sale	−	Ending Inventory	=	Cost of Merchandise Sold
a.	$9,827.71	+	$3,283.72	=	$ 13,111.43	−	$4,823.80	=	$ 8,287.63
b.	$10,552.70	+	$18,722.63	=	$ _____	−	$8,329.72	=	$ _____
c.	$12,350.90	+	$ _____	=	$25,350.90	−	$14,340.25	=	$ _____
d.	$ _____	+	$9,780.60	=	$14,555.00	−	$7,240.22	=	$ _____
e.	$ _____	+	$4,787.90	=	$9,332.77	−	$3,575.75	=	$ _____
f.	$8,275.91	+	$ _____	=	$12,354.22	−	$4,278.09	=	$ _____
g.	$9,875.20	+	$8,450.25	=	$18,325.45	−	$6,333.55	=	$ _____

END OF CHAPTER ACTIVITIES Textbook pages 528 to 530

Vocabulary Skillbuilder

Do the Vocabulary Skillbuilder on pages 528 to 529 of your textbook. Use the lines below to write the term that best matches each statement.

1. _____
2. _____
3. _____
4. _____
5. _____
6. _____
7. _____
8. _____
9. _____
10. _____
11. _____
12. _____
13. _____
14. _____
15. _____
16. _____
17. _____
18. _____
19. _____
20. _____
21. _____
22. _____
23. _____
24. _____
25. _____

Application Problems

1. Do Problem 1 on page 529 of your textbook. Write your answers on the form below.

ACCOUNT TITLE	ACCT. NO.	DEBIT	CREDIT

2. Do Problem 2 on page 529 of your textbook. Write your answers on the forms below and on the next page.

a.

ACCOUNT TITLE	ACCT. NO.	DEBIT	CREDIT

b.

c.

3. Do Problem 3 on page 529 of your textbook. Answer below.

a.

b.

CHAPTER 20

ACCOUNTS RECEIVABLE AND ACCOUNTS PAYABLE

TOPIC 1 ◆ ACCOUNTS RECEIVABLE Textbook pages 531 to 538

Check Your Reading

Use the spaces below to answer the questions on page 538 of your textbook.

1. _____

2. _____

3. _____

   _____

   _____

   _____

4. _____

   _____

   _____

5. _____

   _____

Exercises for Topic 1

1. Do Exercise 1 on pages 538 to 539 of your textbook. Write your answers on the forms below and on the next two pages.

Name _____
Address _____

DATE	EXPLANATION	POST. REF.	DEBIT	CREDIT	BALANCE

Name _____
Address _____

DATE	EXPLANATION	POST. REF.	DEBIT	CREDIT	BALANCE

EXERCISE I

Name _____
Address _____

DATE	EXPLANATION	POST. REF.	DEBIT	CREDIT	BALANCE

Name _____
Address _____

DATE	EXPLANATION	POST. REF.	DEBIT	CREDIT	BALANCE

Name _____
Address _____

DATE	EXPLANATION	POST. REF.	DEBIT	CREDIT	BALANCE

Name _____
Address _____

DATE	EXPLANATION	POST. REF.	DEBIT	CREDIT	BALANCE

Name _____

Date _____

EXERCISE 1

Name _____
Address _____

DATE	EXPLANATION	POST. REF.	DEBIT	CREDIT	BALANCE

Name _____
Address _____

DATE	EXPLANATION	POST. REF.	DEBIT	CREDIT	BALANCE

Name _____
Address _____

DATE	EXPLANATION	POST. REF.	DEBIT	CREDIT	BALANCE

Name _____
Address _____

DATE	EXPLANATION	POST. REF.	DEBIT	CREDIT	BALANCE

2. Do Exercise 2 on page 539 of your textbook. Write your answers on the form below.

Helping Hint: Use the illustration on page 537 of your textbook as a model for this exercise.

Check Your Work: Does the total of the schedule of accounts receivable agree with the balance in the Accounts Receivable controlling account on textbook page 537? If not, check your work to locate your error.

202

© by Glencoe.

Name _____

Date _____

TOPIC 2 ◆ ACCOUNTS PAYABLE   Textbook pages 539 to 543

Check Your Reading

Use the spaces below to answer the questions on page 543 of your textbook.

1. _____

2. _____

3. _____
_____
_____
_____
_____

4. _____
_____

5. _____

6. _____

Exercises for Topic 2

1. Do Exercise 1 on pages 543 to 544 of your textbook. Write your answers on the forms below and on the next page.

Name _____

Address _____

DATE	EXPLANATION	POST. REF.	DEBIT	CREDIT	BALANCE

Name _____

Address _____

DATE	EXPLANATION	POST. REF.	DEBIT	CREDIT	BALANCE

Name _____
Address _____

DATE		EXPLANATION	POST. REF.	DEBIT	CREDIT	BALANCE

Name _____
Address _____

DATE		EXPLANATION	POST. REF.	DEBIT	CREDIT	BALANCE

Name _____
Address _____

DATE		EXPLANATION	POST. REF.	DEBIT	CREDIT	BALANCE

2. Do Exercise 2 on page 544 of your textbook. Answer below.

Helping Hint: See page 543 of your textbook.

Name _____

Date _____

END OF CHAPTER ACTIVITIES   Textbook pages 545 to 546

Vocabulary Skillbuilder

Do the Vocabulary Skillbuilder on page 545 of your textbook. Use the spaces below to write the term that best matches each statement.

1. _____   **6.** _____

2. _____   **7.** _____

3. _____   **8.** _____

4. _____

5. _____   **9.** _____

Application Problems

1. Do Problem 1 on pages 545 to 546 of your textbook.

   a. Answer Problem 1a on the form below.

b. Answer Problem 1b below.

Balance of the Accounts Receivable controlling account: _____

Is the balance of the Accounts Receivable controlling account the same as the total of the schedule of accounts receivable? _____

2. Do Problem 2 on page 546 of your textbook.

    a. Write your answer for Problem 2a on the form below.

_____

_____

_____

b. Answer Problem 2b below.

Balance of the Accounts Payable controlling account: _____

Is the balance of the Accounts Payable controlling account the same as the total of the schedule of accounts payable? _____

Exploring Computers in Accounting
Textbook pages 546 to 548

Check Your Reading

Write the answers to the questions on page 548 of your textbook in the spaces provided below.

1. _____

2. _____

3. _____

_____

_____

_____

4. _____

5. _____

PROJECT 4

CASTLE JEWELERS

Textbook pages 549 to 557

Before you begin to work on this project, read pages 549 to 550 of your textbook. These pages give you general directions for keeping accounting records for Castle Jewelers.

The forms you will need for this project are on the following pages of your Activity Guide:

Forms	Activity Guide Page(s)
Journals	
Purchases journal	208
Cash payments journal	209
Sales journal	210
General journal	210
Cash receipts journal	211 to 213
Ledgers	
General ledger	214 to 218
Accounts receivable ledger	219 to 223
Accounts payable ledger	224 to 225
Financial Statements	
Schedule of accounts receivable	225
Schedule of accounts payable	226
Trial balance	226
Income statement	227
Balance sheet	228

DATE		INVOICE NO.	ACCOUNT CREDITED	POST. REF.	PURCHASES DEBIT

Name _____

Date _____

CASH PAYMENTS JOURNAL

Page _____

DATE	ACCOUNT DEBITED	CHECK NO.	POST. REF.	GENERAL LEDGER DEBIT	ACCOUNTS PAYABLE DEBIT	DISTRIBUTION			NET CASH CREDIT
						EMP. INC. TAXES PAY. CREDIT	SOC. SEC. TAX PAY. CREDIT	MEDICARE TAX PAY. CREDIT	

SALES JOURNAL

Page ____

DATE	SALES SLIP NO.	ACCOUNT DEBITED	POST. REF.	SALES CREDIT

GENERAL JOURNAL

Page ____

DATE	ACCOUNT TITLE AND EXPLANATION	POST. REF.	DEBIT	CREDIT

Name _____

Date _____

CASH RECEIPTS JOURNAL   Page _____

DATE	ACCOUNT CREDITED	POST. REF.	ACCOUNTS RECEIVABLE CREDIT	SALES CREDIT	REPAIR REVENUE CREDIT	NET CASH DEBIT
9	*Carried Forward*		2 6 0 1 00	3 1 2 5 85	9 1 3 50	6 6 4 0 35

Check Your Work: Do your totals to be carried forward agree with those shown here?
If not, recheck your work to locate your error or errors.

CASH RECEIPTS JOURNAL   Page

DATE		ACCOUNT CREDITED	POST. REF.	ACCOUNTS RECEIVABLE CREDIT	SALES CREDIT	REPAIR REVENUE CREDIT	NET CASH DEBIT
19— May	9	Brought Forward	—	2 6 0 1 00	3 1 2 5 85	9 1 3 50	6 6 4 0 35
	22	Carried Forward		3 3 4 5 00	6 0 3 1 05	2 2 1 2 50	1 1 5 8 8 55

CASH RECEIPTS JOURNAL   Page ____

DATE	ACCOUNT CREDITED	POST. REF.	ACCOUNTS RECEIVABLE CREDIT	SALES CREDIT	REPAIR REVENUE CREDIT	NET CASH DEBIT

Account No.

DATE		EXPLANATION	POST REF.	DEBIT	CREDIT	BALANCE	
						DEBIT	CREDIT

Account No.

DATE		EXPLANATION	POST REF.	DEBIT	CREDIT	BALANCE	
						DEBIT	CREDIT

Account No.

DATE		EXPLANATION	POST REF.	DEBIT	CREDIT	BALANCE	
						DEBIT	CREDIT

Account No.

DATE		EXPLANATION	POST REF.	DEBIT	CREDIT	BALANCE	
						DEBIT	CREDIT

PROJECT 4 ◆ CASTLE JEWELERS

Name _____

Date _____

GENERAL LEDGER

Account No. ____

DATE	EXPLANATION	POST REF.	DEBIT	CREDIT	BALANCE DEBIT	BALANCE CREDIT

Account No. ____

DATE	EXPLANATION	POST REF.	DEBIT	CREDIT	BALANCE DEBIT	BALANCE CREDIT

Account No. ____

DATE	EXPLANATION	POST REF.	DEBIT	CREDIT	BALANCE DEBIT	BALANCE CREDIT

Account No. ____

DATE	EXPLANATION	POST REF.	DEBIT	CREDIT	BALANCE DEBIT	BALANCE CREDIT

Account No. ____

DATE	EXPLANATION	POST REF.	DEBIT	CREDIT	BALANCE DEBIT	BALANCE CREDIT

GENERAL LEDGER

Account No.

DATE		EXPLANATION	POST REF.	DEBIT	CREDIT	BALANCE	
						DEBIT	CREDIT

Account No.

DATE		EXPLANATION	POST REF.	DEBIT	CREDIT	BALANCE	
						DEBIT	CREDIT

Account No.

DATE		EXPLANATION	POST REF.	DEBIT	CREDIT	BALANCE	
						DEBIT	CREDIT

Account No.

DATE		EXPLANATION	POST REF.	DEBIT	CREDIT	BALANCE	
						DEBIT	CREDIT

216

Name _____

Date _____

GENERAL LEDGER

Account No. _____

DATE		EXPLANATION	POST REF.	DEBIT	CREDIT	BALANCE	
						DEBIT	CREDIT

Account No. _____

DATE		EXPLANATION	POST REF.	DEBIT	CREDIT	BALANCE	
						DEBIT	CREDIT

Account No. _____

DATE		EXPLANATION	POST REF.	DEBIT	CREDIT	BALANCE	
						DEBIT	CREDIT

Account No. _____

DATE		EXPLANATION	POST REF.	DEBIT	CREDIT	BALANCE	
						DEBIT	CREDIT

Account No.

DATE		EXPLANATION	POST REF.	DEBIT	CREDIT	BALANCE	
						DEBIT	CREDIT

Account No.

DATE		EXPLANATION	POST REF.	DEBIT	CREDIT	BALANCE	
						DEBIT	CREDIT

Account No.

DATE		EXPLANATION	POST REF.	DEBIT	CREDIT	BALANCE	
						DEBIT	CREDIT

ACCOUNTS RECEIVABLE LEDGER

Name *Paul Arnstein*

Address *1010 Jefferson Street, Temple, TX 76501*

DATE	EXPLANATION	POST. REF.	DEBIT	CREDIT	BALANCE

Name *Lucy Childs*

Address *85 Franklin Drive, Austin, TX 78701*

DATE	EXPLANATION	POST. REF.	DEBIT	CREDIT	BALANCE

Name *Carl Cleveland*

Address *1408 Chapel Road, San Antonio, TX 78234*

DATE	EXPLANATION	POST. REF.	DEBIT	CREDIT	BALANCE

Name *Dorothy Emerson*

Address *173 Arlington Avenue, Houston, TX 77023*

DATE	EXPLANATION	POST. REF.	DEBIT	CREDIT	BALANCE

ACCOUNTS RECEIVABLE LEDGER

Name   James Farnsworth

Address   120 Azalea Drive, Waco, TX 76701

DATE	EXPLANATION	POST. REF.	DEBIT	CREDIT	BALANCE

Name   Alice Fink

Address   119 South Street, Dallas, TX 75206

DATE	EXPLANATION	POST. REF.	DEBIT	CREDIT	BALANCE

Name   Louis Franklin

Address   1688 Andalusia Way, San Marcos, TX 78666

DATE	EXPLANATION	POST. REF.	DEBIT	CREDIT	BALANCE

Name   Joseph Garber

Address   1007 Magnolia Street, Austin, TX 78711

DATE	EXPLANATION	POST. REF.	DEBIT	CREDIT	BALANCE

Name _____

Date _____

ACCOUNTS RECEIVABLE LEDGER

Name _____ Jeff Greene _____

Address _____ 105 Bedford Avenue, San Antonio, TX 78211 _____

DATE	EXPLANATION	POST. REF.	DEBIT	CREDIT	BALANCE

Name _____ Robert Harrison _____

Address _____ 2432 Arden Avenue, Houston, TX 77028 _____

DATE	EXPLANATION	POST. REF.	DEBIT	CREDIT	BALANCE

Name _____ Charles Lopez _____

Address _____ 1410 High Street, San Antonio, TX 78203 _____

DATE	EXPLANATION	POST. REF.	DEBIT	CREDIT	BALANCE

ACCOUNTS RECEIVABLE LEDGER

Name _____ Linda Mull

Address _____ 117 Turner Street, Bryan, TX 77801

DATE		EXPLANATION	POST. REF.	DEBIT	CREDIT	BALANCE

Name _____ Marv Rosner

Address _____ 249 Parkway Avenue, Houston, TX 77028

DATE		EXPLANATION	POST. REF.	DEBIT	CREDIT	BALANCE

Name _____ Alex Toth

Address _____ 17 Country Club Drive, Dallas, TX 75201

DATE		EXPLANATION	POST. REF.	DEBIT	CREDIT	BALANCE

Name _____ Roy Venero

Address _____ 812 Lee Boulevard, Waco, TX 76701

DATE		EXPLANATION	POST. REF.	DEBIT	CREDIT	BALANCE

Name _____

Date _____

ACCOUNTS RECEIVABLE LEDGER

Name _____ Suzanne Verba _____

Address _____ 2835 Elm Road, San Antonio, TX 78214 _____

DATE	EXPLANATION	POST. REF.	DEBIT	CREDIT	BALANCE

Name _____ Clifford Waxman _____

Address _____ 481 Dale Avenue, Austin, TX 78701 _____

DATE	EXPLANATION	POST. REF.	DEBIT	CREDIT	BALANCE

Name _____ Calvin Webber _____

Address _____ 3530 Warren Place, Austin, TX 78704 _____

DATE	EXPLANATION	POST. REF.	DEBIT	CREDIT	BALANCE

Name _____ Louise Woods _____

Address _____ 731 Tenth Street, San Antonio, TX 78208 _____

DATE	EXPLANATION	POST. REF.	DEBIT	CREDIT	BALANCE

ACCOUNTS PAYABLE LEDGER

Name ___ Carbo Wholesale Jewelers

Address ___ 722 Davis Avenue, Chicago, IL 60606

DATE	EXPLANATION	POST. REF.	DEBIT	CREDIT	BALANCE

Name ___ Kendall Company

Address ___ 15 Allen Road, Cincinnati, OH 45210

DATE	EXPLANATION	POST. REF.	DEBIT	CREDIT	BALANCE

Name ___ Manila Corporation

Address ___ 89 Water Street, Baltimore, MD 21225

DATE	EXPLANATION	POST. REF.	DEBIT	CREDIT	BALANCE

ACCOUNTS PAYABLE LEDGER

Name _____ *Staunton Company* _____

Address _____ *8305 Lincoln Avenue, Pittsburgh, PA 15221* _____

DATE	EXPLANATION	POST. REF.	DEBIT	CREDIT	BALANCE

SCHEDULE OF ACCOUNTS RECEIVABLE

_____

SCHEDULE OF ACCOUNTS PAYABLE

TRIAL BALANCE

ACCOUNT TITLE	ACCT. NO.	DEBIT	CREDIT

PROJECT 4 ◆ CASTLE JEWELERS

Name _____

Date _____

INCOME STATEMENT

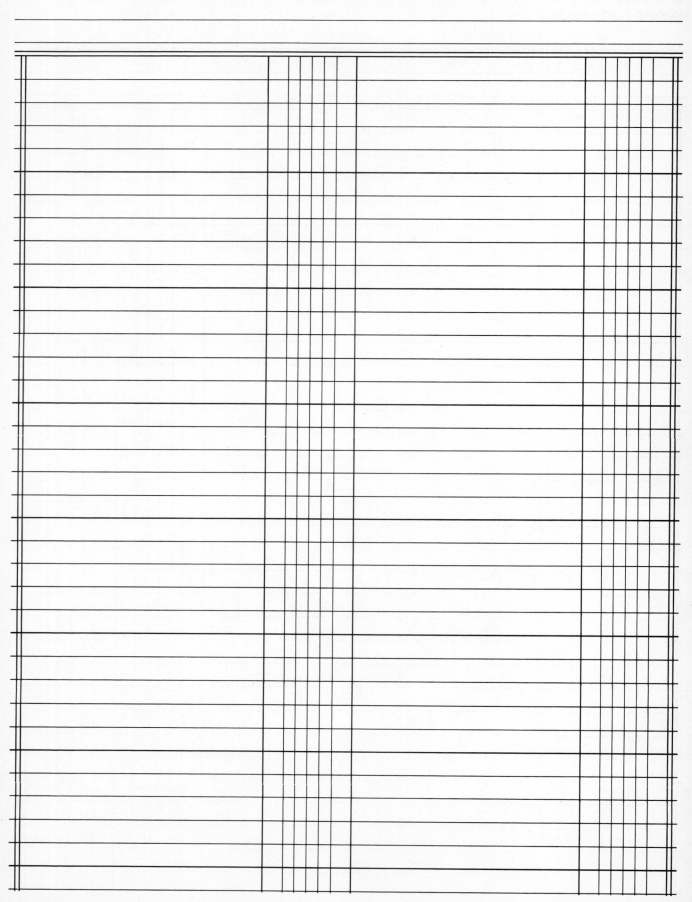

228

Learning Through Practice

There are 30 recordkeeping and accounting terms hidden in the chart below. Circle each one you find. The terms are printed across the page, up and down, and diagonally. Some of the terms are even printed backwards. (For example, "credit" might be printed as "tiderc.") Terms made up of two words may sometimes have an extra letter between the two words. When that happens, just put a line through the extra letter. (Look at the term "balance sheet" on the chart for an example.) The 30 terms hidden in the chart are also printed (upside down) on the bottom of this page. But don't look at them until you have found as many terms as you can. Now start studying the chart. How many of the terms can you find?

```
C  D  I  S  C  O  U  N  T  B  C  D  M  J  P  K  S  Q  S  C
E  C  N  A  L  A  B  C  L  A  I  R  T  N  L  E  D  G  E  R
D  F  C  B  J  N  M  E  R  C  H  A  N  D  I  S  E  F  K  E
M  B  O  W  N  E  R  S  L  E  Q  U  I  T  Y  H  J  A  B  D
B  A  M  X  L  T  V  G  D  T  J  C  I  L  Z  W  B  C  H  I
Q  L  E  T  H  J  O  U  R  N  A  L  N  C  Y  F  R  C  K  T
F  A  F  M  A  L  J  C  N  G  I  P  N  Q  R  R  V  O  G  P
K  N  S  T  L  O  W  D  L  B  N  R  U  T  E  R  T  U  D  S
H  C  T  E  L  S  K  S  A  N  M  M  G  C  Q  I  D  N  H  T
N  E  A  R  O  S  P  I  M  S  E  M  O  C  N  I  N  T  E  N
O  S  T  M  W  P  L  G  B  N  S  N  R  V  K  X  G  J  R  E
I  S  E  S  A  H  C  R  U  P  C  E  E  T  D  L  L  B  J  M
T  H  M  J  N  D  G  D  K  I  R  N  T  Y  F  G  Q  B  G  Y
C  E  E  Z  C  Y  B  C  L  L  T  P  O  S  T  N  G  H  Z  A
A  E  N  P  E  V  F  I  L  O  P  Q  A  M  P  I  N  C  M  P
S  T  T  L  Q  J  A  P  R  Q  K  L  K  G  H  D  E  B  I  T
N  G  Q  E  H  T  J  Y  Q  F  E  K  Q  B  C  A  M  L  F  H
A  P  N  T  I  L  R  C  A  S  H  R  E  C  E  I  P  T  S
R  E  C  O  R  D  K  E  E  P  I  N  G  N  R  H  J  D  N  A
T  W  N  N  H  B  M  H  D  M  C  X  G  K  C  S  Y  R  F  C
```

Trial Balance	Recordkeeping	Note	Ledger	Entry	Cash Payments
Transaction	Reconciliation	Net Loss	Journal	Discount	Balance Sheet
Terms	Purchases	Net Income	Inventory	Debit	Assets
Sales	Post	Merchandise	Income Statement	Credit	Allowance
Return	Owners Equity	Liabilities	Heading	Cash Receipts	Account

Learning Through Practice